MW01252401

"John McIntosh's books and teachings have transformed my life and opened up my soul to incredible heights. His guidance and wisdom has not only brought me material success, but best of all spiritual riches that I have searched for my entire life. Not only has he inspired me, he has helped me find truth and focus from where I needed it most—inside of me. Thank you, John."

 — *Chris Carley, currently number #1 'royalty income' earner in Herbalife International Inc.*

"Inner Guidance is a book of precise and to-the-point methods for creating whatever you may want in your life. Used as a workbook, deep revelations may be released about yourself. Personal power is knowing yourself. This book is a no-nonsense, step-by-step concept of gaining your personal power."

 — *Jodi ShinKara, internationally known psychic and shaman located in Blue Springs, Missouri*

"I am very grateful for your ideas, words of encouragement and the larger vision of what is possible in life. You are a very wonderful and caring person and I am delighted to have met you."

 — *Roger Gauthier, Sacramento, California*

ISBN 1-55212-215-8

9 781552 122150

LIVING ABUNDANTLY
through
INNER GUIDANCE

JOHN
MCINTOSH

INNER GUIDANCE
PUBLISHING

© 1998, John McIntosh. All rights reserved.

You may contact the author at:

Toll free:	1-800-838-7114
E-mail:	john@innerguidance.com
Fax:	613-267-0003
Web site:	www.the-wire.com/innerguidance/indexstage.html

Canadian Cataloguing in Publication Data

McIntosh, John Harold, 1946-
  Living abundantly through inner guidance

  ISBN 1-55212-215-8

  1. Guides (Spiritualism) 2. Spiritual life.
3. Meditation. I. Title.
BF1275.G85M34 1998   131   C98-910839-2

TRAFFORD

This book was published "on-demand" in cooperation with Trafford Publishing.

On-demand publishing is a unique process and service of making a book available for retail sale to the public taking advantage of on-demand manufacturing and Internet web marketing. **On-demand publishing** includes promotions, retail sales, manufacturing, order fulfilment, accounting and collecting royalties on behalf of the author.

Suite 2, 3050 Nanaimo St., Victoria, B.C. V8T 4Z1, CANADA

Phone	250-383-6864	Toll-free	1-888-232-4444 (Canada & US)
Fax	250-383-6804	E-mail	sales@trafford.com
Web site	www.trafford.com	TRAFFORD PUBLISHING IS A DIVISION OF TRAFFORD HOLDINGS LTD.
Trafford Catalogue #98-0033		www.trafford.com/robots/98-0033.html	

10   9   8   7   6   5   4   3

DEDICATION

I dedicate this book to the millions of people throughout the world who have come to a crossroads in their lives and have made a decision to seek 'more' from life.

It might have been tragedy or a deep frustration with life which brought them to this place. Or, perhaps they have been satiated by the world and found themselves still thirsting for something solid, reliable and fulfilling that will not let them down.

Whatever the spark that has caused them to put their 'toe in the waters' of inner searching, is of no great importance.

The die is caste and they have begun the inward search for truth that will lead them to true abundance.

How to Read this Book

My objective in writing this book is to lead the reader to the ultimate source of **How-To** information available: the personal **Inner Guide**.

In that respect, this is a **How-To** book about eliminating the exhaustive search for **How-To** go after what you want in life. But much more than that, it is a very simple workbook and guidebook, that if used with open-minded faith will lead you to a source of profound inner wisdom. That wisdom will open up a world of **true abundance** to you.

Stimulating the **intuitive** aspect of our senses quickens the link with this Inner Guide and for that reason there are passages within this book that are left intentionally **open ended.** This allows the reader to cultivate this intuitive sense while they follow the suggestions in this book and fill in any pieces they feel are missing.

I encourage you to read this book with that in mind. If you feel **something is missing,** for you, it probably is. When that happens, allow yourself to open up to an **expanded explanation** and I believe you will find the book will begin to wrap itself around your specific needs and more quickly lead you to your personal Inner Guide.

CONTENTS

INTRODUCTION 1

1 FREEDOM 5
   What do You Really Want? 5
   How to Find the Essence of What You Really Want 9
   Essence Targeting 13

2 THE SEARCH FOR FREEDOM 16
   The Fish Story 16
   Part One: Feed a Man a Fish 17
   Part Two: Teach a Man to Fish 17
   "The Ancient Success Formula" 18
   The Power of Thought 18
   You Can Have It All 20
   The Ancient Success Formula 25
   Part Three: We Are the Fish 28
   Accepting The Fish as Ourselves 30
   Part Three: "The Missing Link" 31

3   **THE JOURNEY INWARD** 33

     Instant, Mass Communication 33

     What is the Inner Guide? 36

     Awakening to Its Presence 36

     Learning to Trust Your Inner Guide 37

     Who Is Speaking Anyway? 38

     The Trust Game 39

     Our inner guidance system 41

     Our Inner Guide 43

     Out of Sequence Direction 43

     Seeing from a Height 44

     How to Tell Your inner guidance system
        from Your Inner Guide 45

     Working with The Success Formula
        and Your Inner Guide 47

4   **GOING WITH THE FLOW** 51

     The AHA Experience 51

     Comfortable Channels 53

     Overlapping Comfortable Channels 54

     The Primary Purpose of the AHA Experience 58

5   **HOW TO TALK TO YOUR INNER GUIDE** 61

     Never Hang Up The Phone 61

     Your Connection to Direction 62

     Learning to Communicate with Your Inner Guide 64

     Symbol Subtleties 66

     Throw Out the Symbol Books 68

     Search for Repeating Signals 69

     Links 70

     Asking For Direction 71

     Dream Guidance 71

Meditation 72

Readings 75

Page Leafing 76

Code Symbols 76

Conduits 78

Interpreting the Symbols 80

Dream Symbols 81

Inner Guidance Interprets Its Own Symbols 84

6   BLOCKS TO PURITY— "EGO SHIELDS" 88

What Illusions Do You Sustain? 88

The Ego 91

Ego Shields 92

The Power of "They Say" to Control Our Habits 97

Where Does It All Start? 98

The Followers Line Up 99

Giving Away Our Power 100

Real Power 100

Power Must Flow Unrestricted 101

Energy Constipation 102

'Attachment' Blocks the Flow of Energy 102

Letting Go 105

Building Bridges Over Blocks 107

Worthiness, the Door to Receiving True Abundance 107

Breaking Old Habits and Creating New Ones 107

The Power of "Icons" 109

We Can Create our Own Icons 111

Anchoring the Icon 113

7   SEEKING THE HIGHEST IDEAL 116

The School of Life 116

Peace 118

The Power of Detachment 118

Self Reliance 121

The Pure Channel 122

What versus How Thinking 123

From Victim to Creator 125

Chose your Thoughts Carefully 127

You Can Make a Difference 129

Epilogue **132**

52 Weeks of Inner Guidance Inspirations **137**

About the Author **195**

What others are saying about John McIntosh **197**

INTRODUCTION

Abundance is not a dream. It is not a wishful fantasy for the naive and foolish. It is our true estate. Indeed, it is the true inheritance of all mankind. And right here and now we can awaken to this reality and bring heaven to earth.

In this book I have painted pictures and told stories that expose and lift the veil blinding humanity from a world without **limitations** and share the link we all have with a wise and loving ally I call our **Inner Guide**. I share my own experiences with this gentle Guide that has become my constant companion. It has helped me awaken to the true estate of all mankind, which is balanced abundance in both our inner and outer worlds.

For many years I was blessed with material abundance by following the principles of success that I originally learned through the teachings of Napoleon Hill. And while I am very grateful for the security it gave me and my wife, by itself it failed to bring me happiness and a real sense of **Peace, Love and Joy**.

I found myself longing and searching for a deeper meaning to life that could fill the void I felt in my heart. During my quest for success, I became acquainted with many other people like myself who wondered why they felt incomplete despite their material ease. Some looked for the answer in denial through alcohol, drugs and self-indulgence, while a few us looked inward for the answer.

My passion eventually led me into regular meditation and an intense study of Eastern philosophies. Such interest was viewed by most business people with cynicism when I first began my study over twenty years ago but, today, introspection and soul searching is a subject that interests millions of people from a broad range of backgrounds and ages all over the world.

When I began writing this book, I had been an entrepreneur for 31 years and had taught *personal development* for over 25 years to thousands of people. In the last 10 years I have gradually integrated the expanded teachings found from my growing understanding and success working with my Inner Guide. In my personal counseling of people on this new paradigm I have found the recessionary period of the early '90s, which created a great deal of downsizing, restructuring and early retirement, also caused many individuals to begin relying more and more on themselves.

As one example, this *tendency toward self reliance* led to an enormous increase of people moving toward *working from home*. But the feeling of insecurity brought on by uncertain economic conditions did much more. For millions of people, it meant the beginning of *a journey inward* to unfamiliar territory.

The new emerging model that lies balanced between the traditional success formula for acquiring material prosperity and the more esoteric teaching that seeks peace and enlightenment helped me fill the void in my life. I call this new model *The Fish Story–Part Three*. It takes this wonderful metaphor to another level beyond teaching a person to fish and feeding him for life to a new concept that *we are the fish itself*.

It teaches that if we look within we will find material abundance that is balanced and secure together with a profound sense of *Peace, Love and Joy* as we learn we are part of everything; what I call the *'All that Is.'* My life today revolves around this new ideal, and I know it works.

In this book, I will share with you *how to identify, link with, communicate with and trust* a wise and loving source of direction within, which I call our *Inner Guide*. I review the current success creation model of teaching a person how to fish and add a key missing ingredient to the new model, which I call *Passion*.

I explain how we block this connection to our Inner Guide, through what I call *Ego Shields*, then show how to overcome them. I explain how we can go with the flow of life, through a concept I call *comfortable channels*, and allow the Inner Guide to more swiftly lead us to a balanced sense of abundance, both in the inner and outer worlds. And I clarify how a person can identify the goals which will give them a real living experience of abundance. I define this as:

> *"A balanced life, wanting for nothing, and filled with Peace, Love and Joy"* **through a process I call** *Essence Targeting*.

Then I share the grand adventure of confidently *pursuing the highest ideal within* us as a natural next step after realizing all abundance is possible for each of us. The result is to become the ideal, and to become the ideal is *to become a shining light* for others to follow.

1
FREEDOM

What do You Really Want?

What motivates you? What would really make you go out there and make things happen? I want to begin by personalizing this book for you individually by having you answer *four key questions* in the spaces provided below.

The first question: *"What do you lack in life today?"* This is usually the easiest one to answer and is frequently quite lengthy. But for our purposes, try to keep it to the top 20 things. Please do this before proceeding.

1. _____

2. _____

3. _____

4. _____

5. _____

6. _____

7. _____

8. _____

9. _____

10. _____

11. _____

12. _____

13. _____

14. _____

15. _____

16. _____

17. _____

18. _____

19. _____

20. _____

The next question deals with the opposite condition: *"What do you now have in your life that is important to you?"* Please don't skip over this too quickly. Remember, we often take many things for granted that we would miss greatly if they were ever taken away from us. Please list the top 20 things that are important to you before proceeding.

1. _____

2. _____

3. _____

4. _____

5. _____

6. _____

7. _____

8. _____

9. _____

10. _____

11. _____

12. _____

13. _____

14. _____

15. _____

16. _____

17. _____

18. _____

19. _____

20. _____

These next two questions can be a lot fun if you allow yourself to *just let go*. *"In a perfect life, what would you do if you could do anything?"* Please list 10 before proceeding.

1. _____

2. _____

3. _____

4. _____

    5. _____

    6. _____

    7. _____

    8. _____

    9. _____

    10. _____

And while this question may have some answers similar to your last list, it covers a broader range: *"What would exist in a perfect world if you could do anything to change it?"* Please list 10 things before proceeding.

    1. _____

    2. _____

    3. _____

    4. _____

    5. _____

    6. _____

    7. _____

    8. _____

    9. _____

    10. _____

You now have most of the basic ingredients in your hands to live life abundantly. I will discuss the missing *key* ingredient in *Part Three*, but before that, we will need to find the *essence* of what you really want.

How to Find the Essence
of What You Really Want

Hidden within the desires and dreams of everyone is what I call the **essence** of a goal. It is a deep seeded longing that fuels the fires of our most passionate thoughts, words and deeds. It keeps us going when we crave release, rest and peace, because it is borne out of the **heart of peace** where our **true heart's desire** lives.

An effective system to uncover this **essence** within is a technique used for centuries known as the **"not this, not that"** system.

Paraphrasing a familiar statement from Michaelangelo regarding his world-famous sculpture of David: "The statue of David was already hidden within the stone when I began my work, I merely chipped away the stone that was not part of the inner statue and revealed it." True humility to say the least, but which pieces does one know to chip away? The answer: **the ones you don't want**. Sound too simple? Well most direction that **emanates from within truth** is simple.

Rather than looking directly for what we **want**, we eliminate what we **don't want** leaving our true heart's desire, the true essence of what we need and want—**our destiny**.

If this deeper search is not undertaken before we approach what we think we want, then the **joy** we expect to find when we obtain it is never fully realized. We then find ourselves pursuing goal after goal after goal in an unconscious attempt to achieve the deeper **unknown** need.

For example, have you ever said to yourself, "If only I could just get out of debt, I would be happy," or "If only I could lose some weight, life would be more enjoyable." Are these things really what you want or is there something much deeper behind the condition *you don't want* that would truly satisfy you?

Often these things are *fear oriented*. They tend to be things we don't want, things we want to *get away* from. Nevertheless, it is useful to recognize them as things we don't want because that helps to draw us nearer to what we really do want.

The lists you have completed contains the basic elements necessary to arrive at the essence of what will really motivate you to follow your true path in life—your destiny.

The first part of this concept is relatively simple as it involves things that generally dominate the thoughts of most people. As I said, these are the thoughts about things we don't want. Below I've listed some typical things most people do not want. First, review your lists from above and add other things that you do not want in your life.

Over the last 25 years of counseling people on what they wanted in life, over 85% framed their goals in a way that pointed to *what they did not want*. So, for now, our objective is to go *from* what we *do not want*, to what we really *do want*. Therefore, the second step is to find *the opposite* of each item on the above list and frame it in a positive way.

First, add the *things you want to change* to the list, then write *their opposites* in the same way as I have. Your objective should be to say what you want in a *purely positive* way.

THINGS YOU DO NOT WANT *'I do not want . . .'*	THINGS YOU WANT *'I want . . .'*
1. debt	financial independence
2. to smoke	healthy lungs and body
3. my dead end job	a fulfilling, satisfying job
4. my junker car	safe, reliable transportation

5. to live in an undesirable neighborhood — to live in a safe, friendly neighborhood
6. to live in an uninviting house or apartment — to live in a satisfying, uplifting living environment
7. deadbeat friends — to have healthy, fulfilling associations
8. bad relationships — intimate, mature, and mutually uplifting relationships
9. my flabby body — to eat a healthy, invigorating diet and exercise regularly

10. _____ _____

11. _____ _____

12. _____ _____

13. _____ _____

14. _____ _____

15. _____ _____

16. _____ _____

17. _____ _____

18. _____ _____

19. _____ _____

20. _____ _____

Some of the *want* answers may seem conservative at first glance. However, a baby step to the next echelon above what *"you do not want"* is more easily attained than trying to reach for the moon before you get off the ground.

Now lets look at a few of the things you *do not want* and the things you *want* on our list. Go to number #4, "I do not want my junker car." Did you write something like, "Get a brand new red Ferrari"? If so, that may be beyond your *current belief system* and immediately shut down your pursuit of your real need in this case.

Choosing to obtain safe, reliable transportation, however, may currently be within your immediate grasp. There are many fine inexpensive, used vehicles that could provide a very important boost to your belief that you *can* make meaningful and positive changes in your life. In the process of reprogramming your inner guidance system, which I will cover in detail later, small positive changes in your life are fundamental requirements in the process of successfully creating your own reality, a process essential in order for you to experience an abundant and joyful life.

You may ask why I chose *"financial independence"* for *want* number #1. Financial independence to many people immediately conjures up images of winning a giant lottery. But I did not say *independence from finances*; I said financial independence, which is a much different thing.

Financial independence is simply having enough money from the fruits of your labors each month to pay your bills. That figure may be and usually is a relatively small amount of money. Moving to the next step of *independence from finances* is usually still a relatively tiny amount of money, compared to what you may now think.

This amount is actually the same monthly requirement to be financially independent, but in this case, there is no effort as the money is available from the fruits of *past labors*. This may be realized through interest earned on savings, dividends on securities, an annuity, a retirement fund, royalties, or it could come from an inheritance or even a lottery. But, as I said, the monthly amount is not the issue; the ***freedom from working*** for it is. This does not mean you are rich or, more importantly, living abundantly, but it does mean you are free with regard to financial requirements.

That freedom makes you ***independent from finances*** and freedom gives you ***choices***. That is a very important ingredient in the process of living an abundant and joyful life.

Ask yourself this question: If you could work ***because you wanted to work*** not ***because you had to***, and as a result you chose to do exactly the work you wanted to, do you think that would contribute to a more joyful life? The answer is obvious isn't it?

The analogy I am using here confirms the value of creating a new reality through baby steps, which virtually anyone can make in their lives relative to where they now find themselves. They are believable and, ***if believable, they are achievable***.

Essence Targeting

Now, go back and work on your lists pulling information from each as you go. Then, prioritize and sift the list down until you find the thing or things that ***turn you on*** the most.

After you have looked at the thing(s) on the surface, begin to search beneath the surface for what it is that drives your ***innermost passion***. That is where you will find ***your heart's desire***.

As you do this ask yourself: ***"What is the essence of this thing?"*** For example, under the 'I do not want to live in an undesirable house or apartment' category, if you said you wanted a mansion, is that what you really want or is it something deeper? Then, going deeper and being as honest as you can with yourself, you may ask: "Do I really want *recognition* of my accommodation, rather than a nice place to live?" Do you get a sense for where this is leading?

Going deeper still, the next question you may ask yourself might be, "Do I just want to be *accepted and loved*?" This question may be difficult to ask. I know it is for many who already have the mansion, but it is much closer to the truth of what is honestly driving their ambition. And if it leads to real abundance, the painful honesty it may require is a small price to pay.

Try to go through this procedure with as much honesty as you can. If you need to keep the answers to yourself, write them on a separate piece of paper for 'your eyes only.' No one has to know your inner secrets.

This is a very private thing for most people the first time they do it, but very revealing and sometimes, astonishing.

Once completed, if you have given this procedure the sincerity and depth of thought it deserves, you may well have sifted *your essence* search down to the one thing I have heard more often than any.

Of all the answers I have received to this question over the last 31 years, *freedom* is the most prevalent. It is rarely the first answer, but once a person reflects on his or her true inner longing, *freedom* always seems to bubble to the surface as the primary motivating desire behind all the dreams that most people want in their life.

Freedom brings you from the state of *victim to creator* and when that occurs it begins to quickly lead you to true abundance, which is best defined as:

A balanced life, wanting for nothing, filled with Peace, Love and Joy.

This suggests a *state of mind* as well as a *state of being*, an inner as well as an outer abundance. It is almost an axiom that *material wealth without peace of mind is not wealth at all*. On the other hand, how does a person with a *more altruistic*, *spiritual aspiration* acquire a sense of peace if he or she is constantly worried about materialistic needs?

The answer can be found in the next evolution of *The Fish Story*.

2
THE SEARCH FOR FREEDOM

The Fish Story

By following the guidance of the gurus and philosophers of what I call **The Fish Story**, I became blessed with material abundance. While I was and am very grateful for the security it gave my wife and myself, it failed to bring me happiness and a real sense of **Peace, Love and Joy**.

I found myself longing and searching for a deeper meaning in life that could fill the void I felt in my heart. During my quest for success, I became acquainted with many other people like myself who wondered why they felt incomplete despite their material prosperity. Some looked for the answer outwardly through alcohol, drugs and self-indulgence, while a few of us looked inside for the answer.

But before I discuss that inward search, I want to cover in detail what has brought millions of people around the world and over the centuries material abundance, how you can achieve it too and **why it is not enough**.

Part One: Feed a Man a Fish

No doubt you have heard the first two parts of *The Fish Story*. Here's a simple version of the still unfolding story if you haven't heard it already.

It may well have been Day One in mankind's history when Part One of The Fish Story began. Some people who had more than others wanted to help out. The metaphor "give a person a fish" sprang up out of this good work. However, this alone does not solve a person's difficulty since the person in need will still be in need tomorrow.

Part Two: Teach a Man to Fish

Part Two of The Fish Story says "teach a person how to fish and you feed him or her for life." In the last fifty to sixty years, I believe this part really started to gather steam. That's when the growth of personal development, success literature and training programs promoting what I call *The Ancient Success Formula* really started to take flight. Have you noticed how you can't pass through a book store, open a magazine, plug into the Internet, or turn on your television set without hearing or seeing some information about *taking charge of your life*?

The concepts taught through this paradigm have been responsible for millions of people becoming more prosperous when put into use. But *true abundance* in the outer life can only be created if it is first established in the inner life. However, when I discovered the missing link contained in *Part Three* of *The Fish Story*, I found true abundance.

In summary, here are the first two parts of **The Fish Story**. Part One says, "give a person a fish and you feed him or her for a day." Part Two says, "teach a person how to fish, and you feed him or her for life."

The next shift in mankind's consciousness, Part Three, is now quickly emerging.

But before I reveal the simple secret that takes Part Two into Part Three, I want to cover the basics of **The Ancient Success Formula**. Without this critical stepping stone, true abundance is not possible to achieve.

"The Ancient Success Formula"

In order to accurately detail the basic steps of the Ancient Success Formula, we will need to touch on a key fact that underpins its efficacy.

The Power of Thought

As William James said in his wonderful little book, *As a Man Thinketh*, **circumstances don't make the man, man makes his own circumstances**. This means we can change our future inventory by changing our present thoughts. To do this, it is first necessary to discuss the power the mind has to create what it dwells upon.

For me, this mind boggling revelation was the first major stepping stone in my search for abundance. But I had to hear it many times before it finally sunk in. And, do you know when that was? It occurred at a time when I was at **an all time low** in my life, when I was open to anything that could help lead me to a happier existence. It was a time when I was ***totally teachable***. I call this the ***power of humility***. I don't mean meekness; I mean the humility that opens up to the guidance and wisdom of a higher authority.

I first heard about this marvelous creative ability we all posses as a child in Sunday School. I was told that 'we reap what we sow." At the time I did not understand what this meant. Later I read about a great teacher in ancient times known as Hermes who had made the statement "As above so below." This was represented by the two intersecting triangles known by many as the Star of David and also less known as the Six Pointed Star of The Great White Brother and Sisterhood, 'white' in this case referring to purity. It meant that the laws governing the higher planes of consciousness replicate themselves in the lower planes of material form. But I still didn't get it.

It wasn't until my mind was receptive, open and teachable that this powerful life changing truth was absorbed and I understood the incredible potential lying within us all. It was to say the least, a mind blowing experience and one of the best ***'AHA'*** adventures of my life. (I'll cover the power of the 'AHA' experience in Chapter Four.) At that wonderful moment I knew beyond a doubt that I could create my own future life with the thoughts I allowed to germinate in my mind today.

You create your own life and you alone are responsible for it. If you don't like your life, you can change it by changing your thoughts. To know this is the foundation for an abundant life. Once the significance of this power we own really sinks in, we begin to realize that choosing ***'what'*** we think about is of paramount importance.

You Can Have It All

Thoughts are living things empowered with a magnetic influence that attracts people, circumstances, opportunities and ideas to the mold created by the thought to bring it into manifestation.

To illustrate this truth, I'm going to share a story about a remarkable friend of mine, Julius. This story is actually a collage of many stories I have altered slightly and combined to illustrate the incredible truth behind the statement above. If I were to relate all the extraordinary pieces that went into this collage it would require another book.

Julius came from a broken family and was on his own by the time he was fourteen. But he had giant dreams, which sustained him through the hardships and loneliness he faced.

His education and age were against him. As a result, part time, minimum wage jobs were all he could obtain. But the burden of his inadequate qualifications was more than balanced by the scope of his burning desire to achieve great things. When I met Julius he knew nothing of the power of the mind to create, but he had always felt a compelling bond and faith in something within that inspired him to think big.

He dreamt of influencing the decisions of millions of people and wielding enormous influence in the business world. Somehow, he had decided, it would all begin before he was eighteen. He spoke of his dreams to no one and, while he labored in obscurity, the flame of his desire grew. Unknown to Julius, the focus of his burning desire was steadily energizing the magnetism of his goal. And like the potential force building as one pulls back the string of a bow, soon the arrow of that desire must be let loose.

Then, one day the bus he was riding to work broke down en route. Julius could have waited for a replacement bus but, instead, he obeyed a **hunch** *to hitch a ride. The ride he got took him past an automobile dealership. As the driver passed by the showroom, in the window Julius spotted an incredible, shiny new sports car.*

The car was a new concept vehicle just introduced by the manufacturer and that day was the beginning of its pre-launch, restricted to only a few dealerships in the country. The manufacturer wanted to obtain consumer feedback on the car in order to design the most effective advertising campaign before releasing it for sale.

Julius thanked the driver, got out at the next stop and ran back to the dealership. It was early Monday morning and everyone in the dealership was in a meeting. His heart pounded as he approached the amazing car. Never in his life had he seen anything so beautiful on four wheels.

He tried the door handle and it opened with just a touch. He stood back a bit, looked around, then opened the door. He rubbed off the perspiration on his hands down the side of his trousers then stepped inside the amazing vehicle. As he sat down in the driver's seat he immediately heard a soft but distinct voice in his mind speak a single word, **"Destiny!"**

It was a familiar voice, one he trusted and the word made his heart beat even faster. "Looking for a new car young fellow?" A voice behind him asked. "Oh, uh, ya. I mean, yes, sir. This is a beauty isn't it?" he replied sheepishly as he quickly removed himself from the powerful machine. The salesman smiled kindly while nodding his head. His warm manner immediately put Julius at ease, so he decided to ask if he could have a brochure.

The salesman instantly produced one he had been hiding behind his back and gave it to Julius. "I thought you might want one of these," he laughed. Julius took it with appreciation and said he had to be going or he would be late for work.

The salesman smiled as he watched Julius run from the dealership, tightly clutching the brochure he had given him. "Well, that's one consumer who loves this car," he thought, expecting never to see Julius again. He was right about Julius loving the car, but not about never seeing him again.

Everyday for the next three weeks, Julius arrived early in the morning and sat gleefully behind the steering wheel as he imagined himself roaring down the highway in his dream car. He and the salesman soon became good friends as they exchanged accolades about the car's sleek design, unique technical specifications and dynamic handling capabilities.

Julius had learned every specification of the new sports car. He then went on to study its potential competition, visiting dealership after dealership, questioning sales agents about every conceivable detail. He knew every comparable car on the market as if he had designed them himself. He had found a passion which fueled his dreams and he reveled in the exhilaration of the experience. He decided he would have one, no matter what price he had to pay.

One morning the vice president of advertising arrived at the dealership to speak with the sales staff. He discussed the results of the consumer questionnaire reports that had been compiled on the new vehicle and asked for feedback and ideas. Julius' friend immediately piped in enthusiastically suggesting everyone follow him to the showroom.

The V.P. was intrigued sensing something special was about to happen, "Why not?" he said. "Let's go!" Everyone trooped into the showroom and there, as usual, sat Julius behind the wheel of what by now had become his dream car. Everyone laughed as the salesman pointed to Julius. By now he was treated like the dealership mascot and was often consulted on technical details when knowledgeable consumers asked difficult questions no one could answer.

The noise of the commotion distracted Julius for a moment and he turned toward the group of salespeople approaching the showroom. "If you want feedback," the salesman suggested, "there sits the best source you will likely ever find." He pointed to Julius who seemed to fit behind the wheel like he came with the car. The V.P. had a sixth sense for opportunity and his inner wheels began turning as he observed the intense joy on Julius' face. The salesman quickly related all the details about Julius' expertise and love of the car while the V.P. focused on the intensity he saw on the young fellow's face.

He slowly walked over to the sleek sports car and leaned in the driver's window. "Love this car, don't you, son?" he asked. "You bet I do, sir," Julius responded to the smiling executive. "There's nothing like it in the world. I'd do almost anything to have one!" The vice president's smile turned to a wide grin as he drank in the joy Julius radiated.

He hesitated for just a moment then asked, "How would you like to be our spokesman for this new sports car, young man?" Julius could hardly believe his ears. He looked over at the grinning executive in a daze and saw the seriousness in his eyes. Speech failed him so he just nodded his head vigorously. Tears filled his eyes and he began shaking, thankful that he was already sitting down for fear that he may have fainted if he was standing. His dream was about to manifest. He had established a goal to influence the decisions of millions of people and wield enormous influence in the business world. He had set a time limit for the attainment of his target and he had focused on it with a burning desire. But it was not until the sports car came into his life that he had begun working on a plan. That final piece of the success formula had been fulfilled when he began researching the car.

The sports car literally became a vehicle for the manifestation of his dreams. It narrowed his focus and gave all the power of his desire for achievement to the automobile and the industry that lay behind it.

A month later, Julius began his new career as corporate spokesman for the dynamic new sports car. He appeared in a nationwide advertising campaign and toured the country promoting the car in hundreds of different publicity events. And, on his eighteenth birthday, in the showroom where it all began, the vice president handed him the keys and ownership papers to the car he had sat in so many times.

What may have happened if the bus carrying Julius to work had not broken down and he had not been obliged to hitch a ride that took him past the dealership, or if he had waited for a replacement bus that would have followed the regular route?

The magnetic force Julius had built up through his focused desire to achieve great things in life would have found another channel, just as water always finds its level. But it is likely that because Julius had developed a trusting link with his Inner Guide, despite not knowing what it was, he was influenced to hitch a ride. And it was that ride that took him in the right direction, toward his destiny.

Now, here are the basic steps for creating as taught through The Ancient Success Formula.

The Ancient Success Formula

(i) Goals, targets or objectives

You must have a target to focus on in order for *it* to manifest in your life. That would seem to be common sense wouldn't it? Nevertheless, the vast majority of humankind do not have specific goals. They focus on nothing in particular each day, and that is exactly what they get. Would you board an airplane without a destination? Not likely. Goals such as, "being happy," "being rich" or "being famous" are not sufficiently specific to *attract* the condition into your life.

Julius had a specific goal: he dreamt of influencing the decisions of millions of people and wielding enormous influence in the business world. While general in character, it was a specific goal that needed only a specific 'vehicle' on which to focus.

(ii) Time Factor, when you want it to manifest.

On choosing your flight destination, would you accept an agenda that said something like, "we'll get there eventually"? I don't think so. When working with the power of the mind, definite parameters need to be put into place in order to give power to the magnetic force working within it.

It is important to note, however, that flexibility is part of this facet of the success formula. Agendas can be adjusted backward or forward as the goal comes more clearly into focus and begins to take shape.

(iii) Plans, guidelines for the action to be taken.

Once again, would you accept a flight plan that said something like, "Oh well, we'll just sort of wing it till we get there"? That does not instill much confidence that the flight will arrive safely, if at all, does it?

But like your time parameter, and like architectural plans for the construction of a custom-built home, flexibility is essential. As you progress with the building of your dream, opportunities and challenges are encountered and if your plan is not flexible, the successful manifestation of that dream may not be realized.

(iv) *Visualization,* focus.

Energy follows your thought; that is its power. If you were flying through the air toward your destination and the pilot kept turning off the engines, it is likely disaster would soon befall the flight. The same is true of a laptop computer. If you pull the plug on its power source, it will operate for a limited time then shut down until power is restored.

At the very least, your time factor and likely your plan will need constant adjustment in order for the dream to ever manifest. But usually, loss of interest sets in and the dream dies.

(v) *Burning Desire,* your goal must turn you on.

A burning desire is an essential ingredient in the **Success Formula** for your goal to manifest. Without it, sooner or later the following key facets in the pursuit of your dream will be impaired and eventually lost:

Consistency will be lost leading to procrastination

Persistence, the ability to rise above obstacles will falter and die

Balance will be thrown off resulting in discouraging ups and downs in your attitude

Momentum, the compounding effect of small successes that make it easier and easier to achieve your goal as time progresses, will never occur.

Momentum is perhaps the most important ingredient in **sustaining** success. Look at the meteoric rise to fame of many people in the entertainment industry that often leads just as quickly to catastrophic failure a few years later. The loss of **sustained momentum** is one key missing ingredient in these sad cases.

In summary, to achieve anything in life, whether you consciously follow these Success Formula ingredients or not, requires that you know **what** you are going after, **when** you want to get there, and **how** you are going to proceed. These are then combined with a steady **focused attention** and an **overwhelming desire** to achieve what you want.

Think of anything specific you have achieved to date—such as graduating from high school or university, getting your driver's license, learning to bake a particular delicacy, becoming an accomplished musician or gardener or any other dream you went after and reached—and you will be able to trace backwards the Success Formula ingredients you followed to reach your destination.

Nevertheless, with the millions upon millions of accomplishments achieved using this Ancient Success Formula, as it stands as part of The Fish Story—Part Two:

> **This Success Formula is <u>self oriented</u>, taking energy from outside.**

And despite the basic truth and efficacy of this ancient formula, the majority of the world still lives hand to mouth or worse while the growth of millionaires continues, widening the gap between the haves and have nots. This eventually leads to a more dramatic and visible contrast of opulence and poverty.

This condition is partially responsible for many people *ceasing to dream* of a better life for themselves. They *lack freedom* and believe that they can never attain it.

> *Without freedom, living with true*
> *abundance is impossible.*

And for those who have achieved abundance in the material world—without the missing key ingredient in the Fish Story — Part Three—true abundance in both the outer and the inner world is not possible either.

Part Three: We Are the Fish

When you discover *Part Three* of *The Fish Story*, you realize that *you yourself are the fish*. Humankind is quickly awakening to the reality that all we need, we already are. That's right, *we already are.* This means we are part of what I call the *"All that Is,"* or *"the all pervasive universe of abundant potential that exists all around and within us."*

When we awaken to the fact that the *'All that Is'* must also include *us* if indeed it is *"All,"* we soon realize that anything we need must already exist *within us* and *all around us*. To live abundantly in Peace, Love and Joy in both the outer world and our inner world must become a state of our being that *knows* there is nothing outside ourselves.

A state of being is a state of knowing. Before I learned to ride a bicycle I believed such a thing was possible, but it was still only a potential, outside my awareness. I had to experience it to make it part of my reality.

The experiences leading up to knowing that we are the fish, that we are one with the *'All that Is,'* can be quickened by *going with the flow* of our life's purpose. In Chapter Four—"Going with The Flow," I will share a concept I call *comfortable channels* that will help you do that easily.

Once we are empowered with knowing that we are a part of the "All that Is," it becomes possible to *attract to ourselves* both inner and outer abundance by a passionate and concentrated focus of our attention on the *essence* of what we want—our *heart's desire.*

Empowered with this awareness, we know that all inner and outer abundance is already a part of our true state of being, and that there is no distance between it and our passion to experience it. There is no need to fish for it as the fish is within us.

As part of the 'All that Is,' *we are co-creators* who manifest the conditions we want from within ourselves from a higher *state of awareness.* This could be compared to a deeper layer of an onion skin *extending* outward limitlessly. It is still the same onion, only enlarged upon by our focused desire or intent to manifest it.

But how do you move out of the *limited program* that you must fish outside yourself for your needs into the new paradigm *that you are the fish?* I found the quickest way was to develop *a conscious, trusting relationship with my Inner Guide*, which gently directed me to this expanded vision, to this new state of being.

Accepting The Fish as Ourselves

Because I was searching for a deeper level of abundance than material abundance, I quickly embraced this new paradigm on an intellectual level. But because I had not actually experienced it, it was not yet my reality. Understandably, you may be skeptical as I was about your ability to shift to this new way of thinking, and for good reason.

When we go to a movie and watch an action hero go through a series of mind boggling challenges in rapid succession, overcoming incredible odds, rising above torturous treatment finally to vanquish the villain and triumph, we may feel exhilarated and pumped to capacity. Our self-confidence and affinity for the hero may peak, but when our real life confronts us the next day, those hero-like characteristics usually elude us. Why is that? Because we know they are not part of who we *see ourselves to be*. I assure you they could be if that is what you *really want*.

The concept of accepting ourselves as the fish, as a part of the 'All that Is,' *the all pervasive universe of abundant potential that exists all around and within us,* may seem like a dream at best. We might say, "it's just not normal to think that way." However, once we know we are the fish, it becomes extraordinary to us that *normal thinking* includes any belief in *limitation*.

Wouldn't you agree that the concept of lack and limiting circumstances somehow controlled by an outside, unknown force is epidemic? If we want to test this theory, all we have to do is have an "anything is possible" conversation with almost anyone and... well, you see my point! Even the most optimistic person will likely have a "ya, but," or "except for this," to add to the conversation.

And yet, if we are to achieve true abundance on both an inner and an outer level, we must *know* we are part of the all pervasive universe of abundant potential, the 'All that Is.'

> *A balanced life, wanting for nothing,*
> *and filled with Peace, Love and Joy.*

That is the best definition for abundance that I have found.

But how do we achieve a state of knowing that we are a part of the all-pervasive universe of abundant potential? Once again, I became aware of this by working with my *Inner Guide*. It helped me to *go with the flow of my life's purpose* and tap into the higher frequencies of the 'All that Is.'

Part Three: "The Missing Link"

The link missing in Part Two of The Fish Story that takes that concept into a vastly more powerful paradigm is *passion*. The *passion* I speak of is not only an 'intense emotion'—that is the definition of a *'burning desire,'* which is the key ingredient in The Ancient Success Formula, the foundation of the Fish Story—Part Two.

The *passion* I am speaking about is something far deeper and is critical to living a truly abundant life. This *passion* is based on *coming from a position of love* and *unselfish motives* oriented to *selfless service* to others.

> *We do not live in a world that achieves*
> *lasting, true abundance through taking.*
> *The universe is always giving and serving*
> *and because the 'All that Is' is One, that*
> *serving obviously is to another part of Itself.*

Really understanding the reality of Oneness forever eliminates any thoughts of "selfishness" or a "look out for number one" attitude. Imagine the cells in a brain. They are separated physically but, only working in concert, do thoughts occur.

The obstacle to this thinking is that we see ourselves as bodies, not minds, which are in turn facets in One Mind. The body does not think although part of the mind operates through the body as the "body-mind" to facilitate the myriad autonomic functions it must perform to keep the body alive, vibrant and in balance.

We are part of One Mind and if for only an instant we can separate our individual identity away from the body and see ourselves as undifferentiated droplets in an eternal ocean of Mind, we will grasp the reality of our Oneness with the 'All that Is'.

3
THE JOURNEY INWARD

Instant, Mass Communication

More than any other influence today, instant mass communication has caused millions of people to journey inwards for solid, reliable guidance.

We are in an age of instant information overload, which has created a glut of specialists to sort through the maze of variables and choices. As anyone in marketing will tell you, when presented with an excess of choices, a prospective customer will almost always say, *"I want to think it over."* That is a natural response to information overload.

However, the majority of things in the media to think over stimulate fear in most people. Here are some of the most prevalent fear generators in the swamp of data that engulfs us every day:

crime, drugs and violence
world economic swings
earth changes
sensationalism

Whether they are on the streets of our urban centers or in conflict in some far away country, not a day goes by that we do not hear about indiscriminate violence. And drug news fills the cracks of every newscast used as mortar to hold the bricks of chaos in place.

While glowing reports of growth in every sector of the western economy abound, we hear about chaos in Pacific Rim stock markets and CEOs of major banks committing suicide.

Countries that only months before touted their opulent lifestyles are now littered with abandoned luxury automobiles and towns and villages ransacked by runaway, lawless confusion.

We have found that the communication available from satellite technology and cyberspace has brought us instant access to world events. This means the ripple effects of economic downturns in any major world center take almost no time to create a wave at home. As a result, the western hemisphere is constantly involved in some form of *bail out economics* to prevent the ripples in the pond of chaos from shortly becoming tidal waves of depression when they reach the shores of prosperity.

Linked to the world in this way, is it possible to trust any localized, positive economic condition if all world areas are not headed in the same direction?

And, in our daily newspapers, we read about cutbacks, downsizing and early retirement on the same page as lower interest rates and record breaking home sales.

During the late '80s and into the '90s, Faith Popcorn, one of the world's most renowned futurists, predicted an international psychological phenomena called 'cocooning and burrowing' which included a extraordinary increase in movement toward *working from home*. Later, she updated this phenomena by coining a new term, *armoring*.

At the same time, increases in deadly volcanism, hurricanes, tornadoes, flooding, mud slides and erratic weather patterns steadily grew. Add to that the most serious El Nino in recorded history occurred in the 1997/98 season leaving havoc everywhere in its path.

One of the most sought after newsletters of the '80s and '90s was the *Earth Change Report,* published by Gordon Michael Scallion, a futurist whose prophetic insight accuracy is akin to Nostradamus and Edgar Cayce. His international audience is enormous and his predictions about further dramatic earth change activity promotes deep thinking about the continuity of life as we have known it during this century.

Arguably, one of the fastest growth industries is sensationalism, whether it takes the form of television soap operas, supermarket tabloids or television investigative reporting shows. The daily dose of O.J., Princess Diana or Clinton lifestyle media coverage has become epidemic.

Fantasy, exaggeration and comic book journalism create a temporary and vicarious escape from chronic self esteem problems and a numbing distraction from insecurity issues.

Nevertheless, the constant exposure to a saturation of *fear and illusion* based images promotes more of that kind of thinking. *This results in the actual manifestation* of those images into one's reality, since *thoughts are living things*.

The pressing question remains: *who do you trust for reliable, accurate guidance*? Who will lead you with integrity and wisdom while sincerely looking out for your specific needs? Who will lead you to a life of freedom, what I call *true abundance*? Remember my definition for true abundance:

A Balanced life, wanting for nothing and filled with Peace, Love and Joy.

The answer is your own personal *Inner Guide*.

What is the Inner Guide?

The Inner Guide is like the genie within that will lead us to the **essence** of our goals, our **heart's desire**, our **true destiny**. That essence or heart's desire stimulates Passion and leads us to true abundance.

It is our link with *'the all pervasive universe of infinite potential all around and within us'* or the *'All that Is.'* It is our wise and loving guide that awakens us to the new paradigm I've dubbed The Fish Story—Part Three.

It is our creative imagination, intuition, source of insights, hunches, gut feelings and flashes (not the hot ones, although many are). And it can and does come to us when we are open to it.

Awakening to Its Presence

Most people already accept that something is **there**, but they don't really understand what it is. If you're anything like me, you've probably caught yourself saying in hindsight, "If only I had listened to my hunch, everything would have worked out!"

For example, perhaps something like this has happened to you:

You're feeling restless and anxious about something important that you've forgotten. You just can't seem to put your finger on it. In your mind you stumble through a series of possible things it might be, but nothing seems to fit and the gnawing feeling in your stomach continues to grow.

*Finally, **you just let go** of the struggle to remember. Then, a few seconds later, you get the distinct impression of a balloon floating gently in the breeze. This could be a 'picture of a balloon,' the 'thought of a balloon' or just the word 'balloon' popping into your mind, and this makes you think of fresh air.*

That thought makes you feel like going for a walk to clear your mind. You don't actually hear the words, you just get a feeling this is what the symbol means. As you head toward the door, your attention is drawn toward your car keys sitting on a table by the door. You pick them up and decide to go for a drive instead.

You head toward a peaceful, nearby park but, on the way, you feel a strong urge to turn in the direction of a service road which runs parallel to a highway. Moments later you look up and see a large billboard that has an advertisement for a 4th of July celebration on it.

July 4th quickly brings up the thought of birthdays and you immediately remember that tomorrow is your mother's birthday. Your anxiety instantly evaporates as you discover the reason for your restlessness.

Living abundantly comes from awakening to the presence and reality of this wise and loving **Inner Guide**, learning **to communicate** with it and **trusting** and **following** its guidance.

Learning to Trust Your Inner Guide

Who Is Speaking Anyway?

I used to think people with gut feelings and hunches were people with stomach problems and bad posture. Of course, later I learned these terms were slang for the voice of silence, intuition, flashes of insight, inspiration, the still-small voice, or one of the many other names that refer to an innate human faculty I call our **Inner Guide**.

When I first started going inside for guidance, the greatest challenge for me was trusting the suggestions I was receiving as wise, loving and accurate and, therefore, coming from my Inner Guide and not a voice from some other source. I soon discovered the most common source of suggestions other than my Inner Guide came from what I call our **inner guidance system**.

I'll bet that something like the following has also happened to you:

You need to pick up a small inexpensive gift that has been wrapped for you at a downtown store. When you arrive at the store there are no parking spaces. You circle the block a few times and still there is none. Either you must pay the daily parking rate at a lot several blocks away, totaling more than the cost of the gift, then walk several blocks in the rain (did I mention it was raining?), or take a chance and park in a no-standing zone beside the shop.

By now you are all wound up like a top and your gut feeling tells you, "Oh, what the heck, just go for it why don't you." So you park in the no-standing zone and quickly rush into the store. As fast as you can, you grab the package, pay for it and tear out of the shop just in time to be handed an enormous parking fine by a grumpy looking, rain-drenched officer.

What about that gut feeling? How come it didn't work that time? How do you put trust in an inner voice that seems to work miracles one day and drops you over the cliff the next?

The Trust Game

When I was a very young lad I used to play a game about trust with the other children. I didn't see it at the time, but in looking back, I think that is the main thing I learned from it— trust.

The idea was to stand perfectly erect, as stiff as possible, then allow yourself to fall backwards. Another person stood a little behind you and was supposed to catch you around the upper part of your back and shoulders just before you came crashing to the ground like Wyle E. Coyote. Those who had enough trust in the person behind them to remain stiff as they fell until they were caught, remained in the game.

Even if you have never played the game, you can probably guess what usually happened. Thud? Actually that rarely happened. About half way down, the person falling would usually lose faith in the person behind, bend her knees and put out her hands to break the fall.

Our lack of trust in the person behind us was based on what had happened watching or playing the game in the past. Initially, almost everyone who remained stiff to the end did in fact land with a thud on their back. Naturally, this created a mistrust in the perfect potential of the game, and it soon degenerated into a game of who bent their knees last while falling

After that, only the hard-nosed kids with a private, macho agenda remained stiff to the bitter end. I wasn't one of those kids. Everyone wanted to play the game correctly, but the problem was which catcher to trust?

Trusting the voice within is much like that: who to trust because *there is* more than one voice, and the voice we hear *is not always our Inner Guide*. How often have we got a knot in our stomach together with a mind gripping sensation to act on an impulse, only to find we should have done the exact opposite?

If in fact it was the Inner Guide that urged you to park in the no-standing zone, you may not understand the parking ticket you got as a result of following its direction. Your Inner Guide may have seen another much less desirable possibility if you did not follow its suggestion. For example, had you simply headed for the nearest parking lot, your Inner Guide may have seen the probability of you becoming involved in a car accident on the way. In this case though, because of the intense emotion involved, it's not likely the voice was the Inner Guide's.

By the way, my apologies to parking authorities. I am not endorsing the avoidance of legal parking; although I must admit I have done so a time or two... or three...

Our Inner Guide will never steer us in the wrong direction. Its guidance is infallible since it sees our life from above. One way I picture my Inner Guide is to imagine a laser beam shining its focused light down on my life as if my life were a giant CD. It sees all potentialities and all probabilities; then, gently and quietly suggests the best course of action for me to take **moment by moment**.

So, the problem with trusting our Inner Guide is not whether we will fall with a thud if we remain true to its suggestions, but rather **which voice to trust**. How do we know it's our Inner Guide speaking to us? A little later I will share with you several clues that I have found helpful to bypass the emotional impulses generated from our **inner guidance system** and to tune into the true direction of my **Inner Guide** only.

Our inner guidance system

Our *inner guidance system* is our *ego's memory or identity*. In other words, it is the very existence of our ego. You might compare it to a slowly developing photograph which during our early formative years is foggy and indistinct. This picture represents *our self image* and reflects back to our conscious mind every moment of every day a description of *who we think we are*, together with instructions on *how we should think*, what *our actions* or *reactions* to outside stimuli should be, and many other things that make up the way we interact with circumstances and other people, as we move through our day.

As we grow older a distinct outline slowly begins to form on the photograph, and by the time we reach our early twenties, the picture is pretty clear and focused. As we continue to grow older, the picture usually remains only slightly fluid and changes very little, sending the same *images and instructions* to us which were established in our formative years. Our basic character picture is set unless we turn the tables and *consciously* send new information to the photo which will *reprogram* its format.

Our picture also has a *magnetic quality* about it, attracting conditions, circumstances, people and opportunities that are in harmony with its basic programmed pattern.

If our picture is beautiful, it will attract similar conditions which are in harmony with it, and in turn justify the picture, *anchoring* it more deeply into our inner guidance system. If our picture is ugly, we will attract much less appealing results.

I mentioned the image is slightly fluid, sort of like soft molding clay that allows us to change its shape and design or *programming*. But, if we don't remold the clay ourselves, because we don't know we have the creative power to do so, it will continue to flow in the direction of its original design. These designs are what we call **habits**.

If we keep repeating the same old thoughts and doing the same old things, these habits **reinforce** the existing picture and that makes it harder and harder to change them. In other words we, **get stuck** in our ways. I sincerely hope that with the help of this book you will learn both how your **inner guidance system** affects and controls your day to day life and how you can change it to fit the pattern suggested by your **Inner Guide**.

You have the power in your mind right now to change any program within the inner guidance system that you want to. By working in harmony with your Inner Guide, you can begin right away to steadily remold or reprogram your inner guidance system to find both inner and outer abundance.

Many of the changes your Inner Guide suggests will draw more and more beauty to your inner picture each day as you let go of old patterns of limitations. This beauty increases the clarity of your connection with your **Inner Guide**, since it lives on the higher planes of life where all is in harmony and beauty. That clarity helps you remold your inner picture even more quickly.

As your inner picture changes, I know you will come to rely, as I have, on this wonderful friend and ally, and have faith that its guidance is completely wise and loving. The natural evolution of this trust is an increase in **your capacity and acceptance of joy and abundance** that automatically spreads to other people in your presence.

Our Inner Guide

Our *Inner Guide* is a wise, powerful and loving ally that defies accurate description. It has infinite patience and will appear to remain silently waiting in the background until we ask for its guidance. In reality, it is constantly sending us a steady stream of guidance that usually goes unnoticed until we become familiar with the language it uses.

To begin receiving the benefits our Inner Guide wants to give us, *we must believe it exists*, *listen* to what it suggests, and *follow* those suggestions *with faith* despite the initial fight our logic will put up. This means our Inner Guide relies heavily on our cooperation for help.

After I began to trust and follow the advice of my Inner Guide, things that didn't seem to turn out the way I expected no longer concerned me as much. I began to develop faith that something worse had been avoided, or more often that something better was still evolving, but I didn't have all the pieces to that puzzle yet. I just had to give it a little more time and I would see the possibilities my Inner Guide had seen from the beginning.

Out of Sequence Direction

Did you know that most movies are made out of sequence? Can you imagine acting out a death scene before you rescue the heroine? Without this *out of sequence* method, producers and directors would miss opportunities for the perfect shot, lighting or conditions necessary for scenes in the movie. If a script calls for many scenes containing rain, in the absence of a rain machine, the director better take advantage of Mother Nature's rain whenever it happens or those scenes won't get shot.

Our Inner Guide works in much the same way. It takes advantage of out of sequence opportunities it sees coming our way to lead us in the most beneficial direction. This means we must initially go against the grain of what our logic tells us. Society taught us at a very early age to behave in a linear, step by step fashion thinking and actions, and anything that seems out of step or out of sequence may initially feel uncomfortable. Until it does feel comfortable, we must develop the habit of listening to and following through with the directions given to us by our Inner Guide; even though, at first, its suggestions may not make sense.

Can you remember the toughest jigsaw puzzle you ever put together. You know the one, all one color with 5,000 pieces? At the beginning nothing seemed to fit; even the outside flat-edged pieces were hard to link together. Like that puzzle, the pieces your Inner Guide gives you may seem to come in random order that make little or no sense at all. Nevertheless, I have always found the guidance I have been given has eventually led me to my highest good provided I stayed with the puzzle.

Seeing from a Height

Let's say you and I are merrily paddling down a winding uncharted stream in a canoe. Maybe we can see 50 yards ahead at any given time. The canoe moves slowly and rhythmically as the stream flows along peacefully. Sitting stationary in a helicopter above us is our Inner Guide. It can see us directly below, as well as where we have been and where we are headed.

Suddenly, for no apparent reason, we begin to feel uneasy with a hint that something bad is about to happen. We look around and everything is calm, but the uncertain feeling gets worse. So we decide to paddle over to the shore, take a rest and see if the feeling subsides. As soon as we are on shore the feeling disappears. We wonder at the strange unexplainable change and become curious to find out what it might mean.

So, we decide to go for a walk along the shore. About 100 yards into our little hike, we hear a sound like approaching thunder, and around the next bend, we come upon an enormous waterfall that would have meant certain death had we continued downstream in the canoe.

Our Inner Guide *observes from a height* all *probable outcomes* to a given situation no matter how great or small. It then quietly, gently, but also, as in this case, strongly suggests *the best course of action* to take.

Once we get to know it, we quickly find out that our Inner Guide *never demands* that we do anything. Later we learn that the suggestions it gives us are *specific* to *what is perfect* at that moment in our life, including decisions we make now that will affect the distant future. And, our Inner Guide knows *we are part of everything* and whatever it gives us personally is in some way related to *the good of all.* In other words, it always comes from a *win-win* position.

How to Tell Your inner guidance system from Your Inner Guide

Many people spend much of their lives *living in their emotions*, so most of the direction they get comes from their *inner guidance system*. It's like recycling the same old stale air within a house instead of having it refreshed from the outside. In other words, our emotions cause the *same old programs* to play over and over again causing the *same old circumstances* to be created in our lives.

> **Emotionally charged needs lead to gut feelings from our <u>inner guidance system</u>.**

> **Passionate needs attract direction from our <u>Inner Guide</u>.**

Passionate feelings, which I define as unselfish, burning desires, automatically connect us to our Inner Guide and help us to reprogram our inner guidance system with pictures that attract true abundance.

*For example, imagine a mother driving her children home from an evening school play in a blinding rain storm. She receives an inspiration, as **in a flash**, to swerve left at a critical moment and misses a large, unseen, transport truck, saving her life and the lives of her children.*

The *passionate stimulation* of loving concern for her children, while driving under severe weather conditions, *initiated a link* with her Inner Guide at a decisive moment.

Below are some specific differences that I have found very helpful in separating my inner guidance system hunches from the perfect direction given by my Inner Guide.

INNER GUIDE	INNER GUIDANCE SYSTEM (THE EGO)
- speaks with a thundering, velvet voice, powerful while loving	- speaks in a panic with high emotion
- uses much repetition	- uses impulsive feelings
- never demands, but suggests	- presents obsessive urges,

- always presents a win-win guidance
- feels like a friendly mentor
- inspires, lifts and motivates joy and peace

like "I just have to do or have this thing!"
- often influences competitive 'you or them' decisions
- feels like a dictator
- stirs emotions and thrives on chaos

If I am in doubt about which voice I am hearing, I simply ask my Inner Guide to give me another sign or tell me in another way what it wants me to know. And I continue doing that until I am satisfied that the message is coming from my Inner Guide. A quick way to help the Inner Guide do this, which I find fun and easy, is a technique called **page leafing**. I'll explain it and other methods I use to link with my Inner Guide in the chapter entitled, "How to Talk to Your Inner Guide."

Like any new skill, **practice** is required to become proficient. As you practise consistently, you will learn to listen to and trust your Inner Guide. This will yield benefits far beyond the initial risk you may feel you are taking by doing so. I strongly encourage you to **put your toe in this water**. The experience of peace, love and joy, together with a feeling of deep inner security in my life, expanded enormously when I did, and I know with certainty it will for you as well.

Working with The Success Formula and Your Inner Guide

Working with my Inner Guide has influenced me to **pursue an organic approach** to creativity. For years I **kept lists** of everything I wanted to do and accomplish. I had so many different lists I had to keep summary lists of my lists. It got so my only memory was written on scraps of paper. If I lost the papers I would lose my memory. That would have been a scary thought if I could have remembered it.

I'm not saying I no longer use lists, but working with my Inner Guide has taught me **to let go and go with the flow of life**. Unlike the Trust Game I played as a child, I fall straight and tall into the loving arms of my Inner Guide's perfect direction secure and safe in the knowing It will never lead me astray.

If I have an appointment at 2:30 in the afternoon and an unique opportunity appears before that time, I alter my plans and go with it knowing I have been led by a higher purpose **at the moment**.

I begin with **goals or targets** that have been created out of suggestions provided by my Inner Guide. This could be a relaxing, rejuvenating trip into the country for a week. I do not detail the events of the trip, leaving that to unfold as I go. If I want to visit a place or a friend, that becomes part of the goal, not a specific plan such as you might make on a tour agenda.

The next step is **a plan** and here I am very careful not to etch any of this in stone. If I lock my trip into a fixed date, for example, and my Inner Guide sees a week of thunderstorms at that time, either I will go and fail to achieve my relaxing objectives or the trip will be canceled with the same result.

The plan is important because it is part of the **magnetic attraction** of my thoughts. None of us would buy a ticket on a cruise line from a brochure that said "The Royal Palm Line will sail sometime and go someplace arriving when it gets there." That is not a good itinerary.

I lay out my itinerary in **broad strokes** and while the timetable is set, I leave it flexible. I can hear you saying, "Ya, but my holidays occur at a certain time each year and that's it!" If you think that's it, then that's it! But when you develop faith in your Inner Guide, you will learn to trust it. Its suggestions will either come to pass or something even better will occur.

If this is a new idea for you it may sound unrealistic! But I can assure you that it is far better than the uncertainty, insecurity, anxiety, despondency and frustrations experienced everyday by millions of people *without any direction* at all.

The next piece of the creative success formula is *focus*. Visualize a cutting laser beam you are directing at a piece of sheet metal. If you move the focus of the beam all over the metal you will not create the hole you desire. Likewise, you must keep your inner eye focused on your objective to achieve the desired results. Because your objective, plan and timetable are flexible, allowing your Inner Guide to make beneficial changes for you along the way, your initial focus needs to have a somewhat broader beam.

My trip into the country, for example, may be planned for two months from now without a specific destination. As the time draws nearer, I expect to be shown exactly where and when my trip will take place. How?

For example, I might be in a casual conversation with a friend. The subject may not be related to my trip, but my friend may mention a wonderful spot she had heard of while riding on the subway that morning. It twigs my *trip focus* and I mentally make note of it. Later, while leafing through the classified advertising section of the newspaper, my eye falls on a small ad offering a cabin in the country. Once again my trip focus is twigged and I cut out the ad.

The next day I call the number in the ad and find it's in the same wonderful location as the one my friend had mentioned. The cabin owner agrees to send photos and local attractions brochures and within days I book the cabin.

Imagine a life lived like that every moment of every day. Feel the *freedom* of it. Sense the *joyful adventure* of *going with the flow* of an unfolding pattern of life that is perfect for you. That is part of *living abundantly* when we listen to, trust and cooperate with our Inner Guide.

4
Going With The Flow

The AHA Experience

I didn't achieve the knowing that I was part of the 'All that Is' through a spiritual revelation or some mystical experience, *it came to me gradually* through what I call ***AHA experience***s. I love the feeling when I get one of these. The AHA experience leads you instantly to ***a conscious knowing*** of a truth beyond a shadow of a doubt. You know, that feeling when ***you can just see it, you just get it***! This is usually achieved serendipitously through actual experience, but it can also be acquired with premeditation through what I call ***comfortable channels***.

I'm sure you can remember a time in your life when you studied something that seemed to elude your comprehension when all of a sudden, as if in a flash, the ***essence*** of the subject revealed itself to you. Perhaps it was figuring out algebra, understanding the idiosyncrasies of backgammon, cooking a perfect soufflé, shifting gears on a standard transmission, comprehending DOS after learning windows, surfing, reading music, appreciating the subtle beauty hidden within poetry or a host of other challenges to the growth of your awareness.

In those instances, didn't you find the AHA experience came to you prior to the actual successful fruition of the experience. After that, didn't you approach the subject with a fresh new outlook, a confidence that you absolutely could do that thing, even though you may not actually have done it as yet. Athletes call this ***being in the zone.***

For instance, an athlete standing in front of a high jump bar at a level she had never jumped before has ***a knowing*** come over her. It's a feeling right to the depth of her soul that she would successfully jump that height this time. That is a common example of ***being in the zone. It is also the AHA experience***. It was a temporary condition but, having experienced it, once it could never be taken away from her belief system. That is all she needs to take the AHA experience to the next level, a level of total awareness which is the level of knowing that she could do it every time.

Now this doesn't mean we have absolutely no experience with the concept. It means we just haven't experienced the concept at the higher level, but somehow we just know we can do it. As I said before, I accepted the possibility I could ride a bicycle before I had actually done it.

When I began to grasp what it truly meant ***if*** I was a part of the 'All that Is,' ***I accepted 'that' possibility as well***. That was a stepping stone to the AHA experience that eventually lead me to ***a state of knowing***.

Most of us have this knowing when we approach things we are ***in harmony with***, but find we draw a complete blank when we take on something else. There is probably no hard data on this, but I am willing to guess that most baby boomers that have acquired a computer took substantially longer to learn the basics of using it than those born after their particular age group. In fact the younger a person is seems to be an indicator of how much easier it is for him or her to understand the basics of computers.

Comfortable Channels

Not long ago I was in an electronics store standing in front of a laptop computer studying its components on a chart. Beside me there was a young boy whose hands could barely reach the keyboard of the computer to my left. With adept precision his little fingers fairly flew across the keyboard sweeping through commands and bringing up new data faster than I could read it even though I was now rudely staring at his screen with my mouth hanging open.

The salesman behind me watched my amazement with visible humor and probably would much rather have discussed computers with the child than try to get elementary details of the machine's function into my foggy mind. I think you'll agree this is not particularly hard to understand since children today are immersed in high tech, which has become a routine part of their day to day life.

A concept that has become a part of your being, and flows without difficulty or strained thought, word or deed is a <u>comfortable channel</u>.

Your first language is a typical comfortable channel. You spend some degree of thought structuring your written or spoken words, but the process is basically comfortable. Your comfort level relates to the importance you place on the subject and your degree of skill or lack of it in the channel. If you like riding a bicycle and just enjoy viewing the scenery as you peddle along, a high degree of ability is not required and the channel comfort will be high for you. However, if you are a long distance bicycle racer, a high level of experience and excellence in the sport will be essential for you to have *a comfortable feeling* in that particular channel.

Overlapping Comfortable Channels

Comfortable channels overlap and interpenetrate each other. Channels that have a certain *harmonic resonance or similarity* qualify. Another way of putting it is to say that *certain abilities or qualities we enjoy resemble each other.*

If I was a musician I would understand rhythm, beat, tempo and harmony. The same would apply if I was a dancer. I would feel comfort in both channels since there is harmony between several of the components of each skill. But what if I operated a wrecking ball for a demolition company. How important would rhythm, beat, tempo and harmony be to my comfortable channel? By watching anyone perform this skill you would agree, I'm sure, that for them life and death hinges on being comfortable with this channel.

There are thousands of comfortable channels that seem unrelated but have enough similarity to *allow us to jump from one comfortably into the other*. Dramatic career changes are often not so dramatic when we look at them in this way. If you were a courier driver and quit your job to become a stock broker, your friends and relatives might think you had gone off the deep end. But if they looked closely, they would see similarities in the qualities needed to perform the two jobs. Precise schedules, maps or grids, a sense of urgency, and arranging packages or portfolios are a few similarities that come to mind immediately.

It's true, the degrees of expertise required to do the two jobs varies significantly but the *essence* underlying the two functions makes it possible for the two comfortable channels to overlap. As I pointed out earlier, *the essence of a thing is at the core of experiencing true abundance.*

Let's say you are considering taking up the game of golf with the objective of filling some of your spare time with an activity that will increase your feeling of abundance. You don't need to achieve professional ability, you just need enough skill to provide you with *a comfortable sense of accomplishment* when you play.

Before you buy the equipment and spend a lot of money to join a country club, you will want to understand the basics of the game and *your potential* for experiencing joy in this new channel. You could begin by watching several rounds of professional golf on television or by obtaining one or more of the many videos available on the game. The commentary on these shows or video tapes is usually excellent and will fill in many blanks as you study the game. You may also wish to obtain a rule book on the game to refer to as you watch.

Next you will want to see if you already have any of the common talents golfers who enjoy the game have. If you seem to have a few of these qualities you may now have *one or more comfortable channels* in your life that will feel comfortable overlapping the channel of golf making it compatible as well. The key here is that you are looking for *qualities* that bring you *a feeling of joy.*

To do this you simply list a number of qualities players seem
to have in common who enjoy the game. Some of these might
include:

- focused attention
- patience
- precision
- coordination
- ability to strategize
- calm judgment
- ability to recover quickly from mistakes
- bright clothing... (this one may not be critical to success).

Now **overlay** these characteristics on top of any channels
you are comfortable in and look for the matches. I just look for
the **comfortable qualities**. For example, if **calm judgment**
is something you need to have in your work but you find it
strenuous because your occupation is clearing mine fields, that
is a similar quality, but it's not very comfortable is it?

Continuing with your mine field occupation, see what comfortable qualities match up with your golfer list.

CHARACTERISTICS OF GOLFERS	SIMILAR CHARACTERISTICS	COMFORTABLE QUALITIES
focused attention	yes	no
patience	yes	no
precision	yes	no
coordination	yes	no
ability to strategize	yes	no
calm judgment	yes	no
ability to recover quickly from mistakes	there is no second chance	
bright clothing	preferable	n/a

You are looking at one channel in your life and, as I explained earlier, *a concept that has become a part of our being, and flows without difficulty or strained thought is a comfortable channel*. In the case of this extraordinary occupation, *strain* underlies almost every quality of the job. So despite the *similar qualities* we possess in our work compared to the happy golfer list, these channel qualities *are not comfortable*.

You don't need to look much further to figure out that these particular characteristics may have the opposite effect you want to achieve by taking up the game of golf. Why is that? Because there is a *subconscious connection* to strain connected to these attributes that will bubble to the surface when you begin playing the game for real.

When you finish this review you will have a good idea of whether or not you possess enough *similar and comfortable traits* in areas of your life that will easily expand your sense of abundance in the new channel you want to explore. If you do not find enough similar and comfortable traits and as a result decide not to pursue this new channel, then you are *going with the flow of your life*.

This practice is a *stepping stone system* for *going with the flow* of your life pattern or destiny. But once you *consciously connect* with your Inner Guide, you will regularly know *in a flash* which way the flow is going without going through this or any other procedure to find it.

In the meantime, this is a simple and effective method to determine what channels will be the most comfortable for you to explore in order to experience more abundance in your life. Now, it's true, *you may decide to go against the flow* and proceed with a new channel that is not in harmony with your life. With some struggle and discomfort, if you persist, you may overcome the lack of harmonic resonance and go on to create a new comfortable channel.

The 'All that Is' provides us with innumerable opportunities to rediscover or remember our Oneness with it. But not all the same opportunities exist at the same time for each of us. If we recognize and go with the flow of the opportunities that are available to us at a given time, *life becomes far more joyful* and leads to awakening much faster.

The Primary Purpose of the AHA Experience

Using this stepping stone system, allows you in some instances to encounter the AHA experience before the actual experience takes place, like the athlete who is *in the zone* before the jump.

But for most people, the AHA experience will happen gradually as the harmonizing qualities of *existing comfortable channels* link with *new channels*. These small successes lead to a sense of joy. But while the individual AHA experience felt in the new *overlapping comfortable channel* is joyful and a goal worthy of your most sincere effort, it is not the most important thing worth pursuing.

What is important is the *awareness* that you are a part of the *'All that Is.'* That knowing opens the door for you to experience completely a balanced abundance both in your inner and outer life. You could spend a lifetime expanding the channels of comfort that give you a sense of abundance and it would be like emptying the ocean with a teaspoon. Regardless of how satisfying that exercise may be, it pales when compared to the larger view of life's potential that opens to you when you know *you are the fish.* Instead of *having a point of view*, you have *a point to view from* that shows you that *all possibilities* are open to you.

To become aware that you are the fish, is to become aware of your Oneness with the 'All that Is.' This allows you to *point the focus of your inner vision* at any channel you desire and know instantly *that it is possible* for you to attain it and *that it will be comfortable*. In this state of knowing, *all things are possible to you now*.

When I was a small child I had a recurring dream of having *a machine that built machines*. It took four decades to interpret that dream and unravel the simple truth my Inner Guide was showing me. The machine that built machines is the 'All that Is' and you and I already possess Its power because *we are It*.

How often have you heard or perhaps said yourself, "My God, what a heavenly experience that was," in relationship to *an ecstatic encounter* within a comfortable channel. It may have been a faultlessly executed golf shot, a win-win contract negotiated, a perfectly performed skating routine, a concerto flawlessly played with a depth of spirit, a garden created with exquisite harmony and balance, a reverent hymn sung which moved the hearts and souls of the entire congregation, a piece of architecture consummately blended with the environment while filling its purpose impeccably or thousands of other events that *felt perfect*.

You were not exaggerating, were you? It was *truly an altered state of consciousness* that temporarily touched the 'All that Is' or what was called *'the face of God.'* That is how John Gillespie Magee Jr., a Royal Canadian Air Force pilot during World War II, described it in a poem he wrote about flying not long before he was shot down and killed. No one who has ever, even once experienced such an altered state of consciousness will deny that experience transcended all other worldly encounters.

And this is why I say *we must feel*, not just *know about* something before it becomes part of our knowing.

When we think about the possibility of *a constant flow of ecstatic feelings* as a continuous expression of life, what goal, what ideal, what aim could take precedence over it? This is the true life we have left behind through *the fall of our awareness into the belief in limitation*. But the end of our collective bondage is fast approaching and *we may speed this process* for ourselves and others by learning to *accept the hand that is extended* down to our consciousness from the 'All that Is.' That helping hand is called our *Inner Guide*.

Living our life within comfortable channels creates the potential for frequent heavenly experiences. The repetition of these blissful experiences leads naturally to a state of knowing that the *'All that Is' can be found within all comfortable channels* because we are in harmony with it. Then, sooner or later, it awakens us to the knowing that we are One with the 'All that Is.'

By going with the flow of life, we will connect with many comfortable channels and experience blissful abundance in many aspects of its infinite reality. And by focusing on connecting with our Inner Guide as our *primary comfortable channel*, we will be led to many ways and means that will speed up *the reawakening process* to our Oneness with the 'All that Is' from which flows all abundance.

5
How to Talk
to Your Inner Guide

Never Hang Up The Phone

Keep the Channel Open

If you don't believe your Inner Guide actually exists, or if you feel perhaps it might exist but likely has very little value to you, then you're right, it won't. But I very much encourage you to give it a chance and allow the possibility that *flashes and insights* may be useful to you. I assure you, that if you will do this, your Inner Guide will be very active in your life. Think of any intimate relationship you have successfully developed in your life and use that as a model for developing a close relationship with your Inner Guide.

What if you received a hunch that the weatherman's sunny prediction today just doesn't feel right and you decide, "What the heck, I'll take an umbrella to work with me just in case." A few hours later there is a thunderstorm. This successful hunch is bound to get your attention isn't it? You might decide it was just a coincidence, but I invite you to build on any insight that pans out and open your mind to others.

Each time you open up to the possibility of wise, Inner Guided direction, you make it easier for you and your Inner Guide to become comfortable with each other. Then, as you receive a steady flow of guidance from your new friend, *act on it* and you will reprogram your inner guidance system to work *with* your Inner Guide. This is what I call *never hanging up the phone*. I believe it is also what was meant 2,000 years ago when we were encouraged to *pray without ceasing*.

Your Connection to Direction

Faith increases the connection to your Inner Guide

The programs in your *inner guidance system*—your ego's identity—are as diverse as the grains of sand on a beach. They influence the *faith or skepticism* you have in your *Inner Guide* and influence your ability to clearly tune into and understand the messages it sends you.

Everyday we see signs and symbols posted everywhere: on street corners, highways, the stock market, medical supplies, electronic components, gauges, meters and a host of other locations, sometimes practical, sometimes obscure, that give us direction, warn us of potential danger, guide us to opportunities, describe what lies ahead and, in general, make suggestions that will benefit us. We would be foolish to ignore them, and might even bring harm to ourselves if we did.

Your Inner Guide is *constantly giving you signs* in the same way. It can provide benefits to you, or warn you of possible or probable dangers. These signs are far more accurate and specific to your needs in life than the signs indicated above.

They could be **simple signs** that help make your life easier in thousands of ways, such as helping you find your house keys or remembering an old friend's name. But they can also be ***dramatic warnings*** that can give you a powerful insight that urges you to miss a flight that later crashes, or have you check your brakes just before an emergency situation that would have caused you serious injury.

They can ***save you from untold grief*** and ***guide your attention to opportunities*** that attract all manner of abundance into your life.

When I first started working with my Inner Guide, my faith in it was a little shaky. I'd trust it with small things, like choosing a movie or buying a book, but I had trouble with the big things. If I had booked a holiday and got the impression I should not take the flight, I would have gritted my teeth and got on the plane. I don't think I was put to a test like that, but I may have been and didn't know it.

Our Inner Guide knows exactly how much faith we have in it and will adjust its guidance to fit that trust. So how would it handle the doomed flight warning like the one I just described? Here is one way it might save me from disaster. A small hunch that I might have obeyed would have been to take a different route to the airport. My Inner Guide would have known that on the way there would be a traffic jam to delay me long enough to prevent me from making my flight.

I would be pretty frustrated at missing the flight and annoyed at myself for listening to the hunch, but not for long. This is a dramatic example to be sure but the event, had it occurred, would have left an equally dramatic impression on me. Thus, my faith in my Inner Guide would have increased significantly.

As you become better and better acquainted with your inner source of loving and perfect guidance, I urge you to make it your first goal to develop a deep faith in its wise and gentle guidance. *Faith increases your receptivity to your Inner Guide; doubt reduces it.*

Learning to Communicate with Your Inner Guide

The Symbol Search

Recently, I obtained a new laptop computer and wanted to add a program to it that would allow me to speak to anyone in the world. When I bought the necessary program, I found a compact disk in the package. I learned that the disk held 65 mega bytes of information. If I had to input that information into my computer on my own, without the help of a CD, it would have taken three-and-one-half years, working 24 hours per day, 365 days a year at a typing speed of 70 words per minute. Since I am a two finger typist nowhere near 70 words per minute, I chose the compact disc!

Our Inner Guide works much like a compact disk, only faster. Like the compact disk, words are very limiting and restricting to a guide that sees the whole picture, which includes *the totality of our life, past, present and probable future.* Instead of words, our Inner Guide speaks to us in symbols that can show us its meaning in a single flash.

I also like to think of my Inner Guide as a remarkably accurate satellite which sees weather patterns coming into my life. It can warn me of impending storms or inspire me to pursue gentle and invigorating conditions in another location. This *helps prepare* me to make the best possible decisions for my future. A really important thing I learned early in my work with my Inner Guide was that it sees *probabilities*. If we apply sufficiently powerful thoughts on these probable events, soon enough, *it is possible* for those future events to change.

Your Inner Guide also sends you the same message many times, but in different ways. It operates much like Mother Nature, which ensures the survival of a species by creating an abundance of seeds or eggs to be fertilized. Although many of the seeds and eggs will perish, enough will survive to perpetuate the species. The same is true with your Inner Guide. Most people fail to recognize, understand or heed the signs they are given; therefore, many different signs and symbols are given to communicate a message to you. In that way, the possibility increases that one or more of those signs or symbols will reach you.

We've all experienced *hunches* or *gut feelings* from time to time, which helped us to do exactly the right thing, at exactly the right time, and in exactly the right way. I certainly welcomed those flashes of insight before I knew where they came from. Once I learned this wonderful direction was available to me and *could be tapped into at any time* if I chose to develop it, I became very excited.

One of my first mentors once told me that 75% of suffering is unnecessary. That really got me thinking. I took a serious inventory of my life and recalled the many wrong turns, blind alleys and unfortunate choices I had made. Despite the eventual successes I achieved, each journey could have been much shorter and far more enjoyable if I had just known about and been open to receive *inside* information about how to proceed correctly along the way.

Your Inner Guide is a kind and loving friend that will gently nudge you in the direction with *the least discomfort* and *most joy*. If you let it, your Inner Guide will constantly lead you to **channels of peace, love and joy** flowing to other channels that are just as comfortable, as smoothly as a relay racer passes his baton to the next runner. The reason we resist this wonderful friend's help has to do with the **shields the ego uses** to defend itself and its false identity. Later, I will discuss those shields and show you how to **build bridges over them**.

Symbol Subtleties

Our Inner Guide attempts to get our attention far more often than we may believe, but for many people those attempts are met with skepticism, logical argument and confusion.

Here's an amusing story that happened to my wife and me that I think will show you what I mean.

Years ago, my wife, a friend and I toured Europe in a car we had rented for the trip. When we arrived in a new town or city along the way, we would ask the local merchants for directions to a good Bed and Breakfast rather than consult a travel brochure. As we motored merrily along our way, this proved to be a very satisfactory method for securing a place to stay and enjoying a satisfying meal in the morning. If you have ever done this, you know what I mean.

Most of the towns and villages we visited were quite small, so asking a few shopkeepers or restaurateurs for advice was all we needed to do to secure a comfortable location for the evening. But when we arrived in the larger city of Munich, we decided to drive to the airport and ask at the information desk on the arrivals level for advice in order to quickly narrow down the multitude of choices available in that city.

We found a very cheerful, old fellow dressed in full German lederhosen behind the desk and explained what we were looking for. He immediately replied in very broken English that he knew of a splendid hotel. Our delight at his encouraging reply soon turned to confusion and frustration as he kept repeating that he knew of a splendid hotel when we pressed him for the name.

With a cherubic grin on his face and abundant enthusiasm, he brought out a street map and began highlighting the way to this splendid hotel, only a short drive from the airport, but apparently with no name. Our frustration seemed to escape his attention as we pressed him for the name of the hotel. We volleyed back and forth like that for several minutes trying to get **him** *to understand that we certainly could not find our way without the name of this splendid hotel he was extolling.*

Finally, a co-worker came by the information desk and noticed the language problem we were having. He chatted in German with the kindly old fellow for a moment; then, with a roar of laughter, blurted out that the name of the hotel was 'The Splendid Hotel' and assured us it was as good as its name implied. We all had a wonderful laugh about **our** *misunderstanding, and after thanking the two attendants, headed towards what turned out to be the best accommodations we enjoyed during our entire trip.*

Our Inner Guide uses every device at its disposal to get through to us. It is very repetitive in its attempts to drive home a certain point since most of us fail to recognize the language it uses. But the symbols it uses to communicate with us are as simple as the subtle difference between a **splendid hotel** and **The Splendid Hotel**. As we learn to open our minds, pay attention and listen with a different set of eyes and ears, we will soon understand those differences.

Throw Out the Symbol Books

Symbol books usually attempt to interpret your dreams with *pat definitions* for specific symbols. The simple reason these definitions are not often correct is because our Inner Guide always works with the programs that exist in *our own personal inner guidance system*, which differs greatly from person to person.

If you were an airline pilot and had a dream about falling, it would suggest something entirely different to you than the same dream might suggest to a stock broker. Or if I were a brain surgeon, a symbol of a road map would likely represent something much different to me than it would to someone who makes textiles for a living.

If you've ever listened to a dynamic speaker you probably noticed she used words and pictures the audience could easily relate to. If she were speaking about the economy to an audience made up of country people, her words and metaphors might be full of symbols connected to growing things. But if she were speaking on the same subject to a group of workers in an automobile plant, she might paint images of teamwork, timing and tight profit margins.

Our Inner Guide is the *quintessential communicator* and knows exactly what symbols are most likely to be recognized and understood by each of us. The *easier a symbol is to identify with*, the *more likely we will notice it and, hopefully, act upon it.*

Even if we completely *reject the notion* of a wise inner authority, as I once did, we will still be guided to what is best for our personal growth and welfare, but the route we take will likely be much longer and less joyful. In addition, our Inner Guide *does not need to be recognized or accepted* for its guidance to be useful, although, we will grow far more quickly and comfortably once we work in concert with it.

Search for Repeating Signals

If you were a person who had absolutely no faith in the existence of an Inner Guide and you began to notice a symbol that repeated itself over and over again, I'm sure you would agree that it would be difficult to dismiss. And then, if some event followed the repeating symbols that seemed linked to them, that would certainly leave you wondering what was going on, wouldn't it? This is a common occurrence today as more and more people begin **sensing an unseen force** guiding their lives.

Here is an example of how it works for someone who has begun working with his Inner Guide.

Let's say this fellow is strolling down the sidewalk and hears the crash of a window pane in a nearby house. It gets his attention, but is quickly lost in the steady stream of thoughts we all experience from moment to moment. Later, as he returns home, a bicycle falls over with a crash in his driveway. That gets his adrenaline pumping for a moment, so he stoops down and picks up the bicycle and heads for the front door.

Since this man had begun listening to his Inner Guide, this second crash would have extended his mental antennae a little and got him thinking about what the connection might be. After dinner, he turns on the television and right away there is a crashing sound on the show. Now, he becomes very alert and starts searching for a link.

Links

Links are symbols that seem unrelated, but are part of a story that your Inner Guide is trying to weave for you.

Let's say he immediately turns off the television and sits down to ponder the meaning of the three crashes. At that moment, he is making a conscious attempt to tune into his Inner Guide. Although the station may be full of static, a definite channel for communication exists and symbols sent by his Inner Guide are much easier to access after that.

Our friend now pays particular attention to anything that seems to jump out at him. He casually picks up the paper and opens it anywhere. Immediately, his eyes fall onto a photo of a bear in a cartoon. Since he has practised looking for links, that clue helps him connect the two symbols. Let's cut to the chase and go to the stock market pages of the newspaper where he looks up a blue chip, high-tech stock that holds a considerable amount of his investment capital. He finds it stable just as his broker told him it would be before he bought it. However, his Inner Guide is still at work leading him to its wise direction.

By now he is totally open and receptive to his Inner Guide and when that happens external symbols are often replaced with flashes of insight that complete the story instantly. In this case, he may get the distinct impression that he should go to the Internet and check out what is happening with the company.

*He obeys the impression and finds a late breaking news flash that indicates the company became embroiled in a lawsuit over software copyrights just after the stock market closed. He realizes this will likely mean a large drop or **crash** in the stock, so he immediately leaves a message on his broker's voice mail to sell his shares when the market opens.*

The next day he finds his sell order was completed just before a major crash in the stock. This saves him a significant capital loss.

Sound unbelievable? Well, it's not! When you begin to cooperate with your Inner Guide, it will help you with far more than economics, no matter how important the subject may be to you.

Asking For Direction

If you believe that something lies within you which can make your life better, the best way to obtain information from your Inner Guide is *to simply ask for it*. There are many ways to ask, and you will develop your own as you get into the flow of this new channel and it becomes comfortable to you. First, I'll give you a few of the more common methods I have found that work for me, then, I'll show you how to interpret them.

Dream Guidance

This is a method you can test tonight if you wish. Just before you go to sleep, ask your Inner Guide to give you guidance on something that really interests you. It's also good to pick something you can check out soon after you get direction. Proof that this is working will help build your faith in it.

The question might be as simple as asking when you will receive a phone call you have been expecting, or it could be something as practical as where you can locate an ingredient for a recipe you just can't seem to find.

Have a piece of paper and pen beside your bed in case you wake up in the middle of the night with an insight. Write down whatever you get right away. Don't try to figure it out then; just go back to sleep and look at it again the next morning when you have a quiet moment. If you don't get anything in the middle of the night, you might receive something as soon as you wake up. Once again, write it down and look at it when you can allow its meaning to reveal itself to you without distractions.

If this doesn't work the first time, or even the first several times, don't be discouraged. *Creating a new comfortable channel* is sometimes like digging an irrigation canal to an orchard. You dig, and dig, and dig, and no water flows to the orchard until the last shovel full of dirt is removed; then the floodgates open.

You are *rewriting programs* in your inner guidance system that have prevented access to and from your Inner Guide for most of your life, so keep faith and persist. I assure you your efforts will be rewarded.

Meditation

Inner Guidance during waking hours can be achieved through *a state of inner quiet* called meditation. Of all the methods of consciously communicating with the Inner Guide, this is by far my favorite. It opens many other doors far too numerous to mention here and is the subject of many good books and workshops. I will give you a simple overview of this valuable method and suggest that you conduct deeper research if it feels like this may be a comfortable system to help you make a connection with your Inner Guide.

I have heard about, studied and tried many different ways to meditate; none are etched in stone and most do not require long years of study and practice to master. You can begin today and become very comfortable in this channel within 30 days.

All of us have experienced a form of meditation in our lives, but we may not have recognized the event as such. Do you remember the most boring classes you took in school? Do you remember daydreaming in any of those classes? Well, that was very close to **spontaneous meditation**. It can be brought on through exhaustion, indifference to your surroundings, or fascination with a particular idea or subject.

On the other hand, you can also experience a form of **daydream meditation** as a result of a deep interest in something. Have you heard of inventors **spacing out** during waking hours, caught up in the flow of concepts they are pursuing or inspired by new ones?

There is a very funny story about Albert Einstein walking across the courtyard at a university where he was a professor. He stopped a student on the way and asked him a curious question, "Which way did I just come from?" The astounded student replied, "That way professor," pointing behind him. Einstein pondered the answer for a moment then nodded his head in appreciation, "Oh good, that means I had lunch!" Now that certainly qualifies as spacey, don't you think?

During these episodes there is a clarity that transcends ordinary consciousness and, like night-time dreams, often seems to last for hours. Usually they last only a few minutes in terms of our time-space reality. They flow in the **no time-space** consciousness of a higher vibration where our Inner Guide resides.

You can create peaceful and wonderful images in your meditations. You may want to visualize a quiet, undisturbed setting, but not so comfortable that you fall asleep. Then, with slow, steady, deep breathing, allow your thoughts to flow without interruption or judgment as if you were passively observing someone else's thoughts.

I like to create a peaceful environment, such as a garden or temple, which I regularly visit in my mind during these wonderful journeys inward. Usually, I am joined by wise and loving guides. I ask them specific questions that concern me, or if there is nothing in particular on my mind that day, I use the experience to just relax and rejuvenate. There are no limits within the meditative state since you create your own unique reality with your thoughts.

What would you do if you could do anything, is a good question to ponder during your meditation. With this attitude, your creative imagination will begin to expand and spill over into your day to day reality.

A common practice that I use in my daily meditations is to meet in a placid setting, a group of personalities that have inspired me in my life, living or passed on. Usually, I go to a light-filled temple and lay out before these loving elders my concerns, inspirations and plans for the day. Each one represents wisdom, love or power in one or more of their many facets through which my Inner Guide can send me direction. In this way, it often feels like the personality himself is giving me the guidance.

This type of meditation has been a wonderfully uplifting and peaceful experience for me over the years and has evolved into a constant, helpful dialogue during my non-meditative state. It has become my way of *never hanging up the phone*. If you do decide to use this system to link with your Inner Guide, a conscious connection will occur much more quickly than through night-time dreaming. Meditation has many other benefits that will help you quickly experience more abundance in life, and I strongly recommend a serious investigation into this ancient and powerful practice.

Readings

Readings are an enjoyable way to link with your Inner Guide. They can be done on your own or with a friend who is receptive. Here is how they work. When you first try this method, choose a question that can be verified quickly so you can boost your faith in your Inner Guide when you get results.

Write the question at the top of the page, and if you are doing this alone, begin writing down anything that pops into your mind. Do this **with an easy flow** and **no judgment as to whether it will work** or not. *It is important not to stop and review anything you receive until you 'feel' you are done*, since that will break the flow of your connection with your Inner Guide.

When I first tried this, I felt a little foolish since many of the words, sentences or symbols seemed silly, even childish. You may have a tendency to feel that way too, but stay with it and just let that thought pass out of your mind and continue until you feel you are finished.

If you are doing this with someone else, one person can act as questioner and the other as reader. This method allows the questioner to prompt the reader with off-shoots of the question and stimulates the reader to attract more symbols to help reveal the answer. Sometimes the symbols turn into sentences, so it is a good idea to use a tape recorder to be certain you don't miss anything.

Once again, let go of the natural tendency to reject anything you get as nonsense. I assure you, once you learn to interpret your Inner Guide's messages, it will reveal a wealth of valuable information to you. Just go with the flow and let the process evolve. I know you will soon be pleasantly surprised at how accurate and useful the guidance is.

Page Leafing

This is a quick way I use to verify messages I receive when I am not sure if they came from my Inner Guide. This is a simple and quick procedure involving the use of any book, magazine or newspaper. It works like this: Think of a question and focus on it steadily for a few moments until it is *your dominant thought*. Then take your book or magazine and fan the pages until you feel like stopping. Sometimes I find my thumb just stops at a page on its own. With a newspaper, just turn the pages.

When you stop, open the book and allow your eyes to fall on the first thing that attracts you. *Don't force this, just allow it to come to you*. This may be a single word, the beginning of a sentence, or a paragraph. Read as little or as much as you sense you should and then close the book. If you wish, write down the word or dominant theme of the passage. This is the beginning of the answer.

Code Symbols

Over the years, I have developed a few code symbols with my Inner Guide that I use as a reminder that my loving friend is with me. I also interpret them as confirmation that an insight received has indeed come from my Inner Guide, and not my inner guidance system. I see one of these code symbols at least once or twice every day. *It is the number 1122*, or the number 2211. In the ancient practice of numerology, these numbers represent power in various forms.

I will be driving down the highway and glance at a license plate and the numbers will be there. I will look at a digital clock just as the numbers change to 11:22. Or, I may see it on a T-shirt, in a magazine, or on a bar code on the side of a box of cereal.

I mentioned this to my sister years ago when we were in a workshop waiting for a closing dedication. Each of the students had drawn a number so that a technician could link our dedication to tape recordings she was making for us.

My sister and I sat in a circle opposite one another and she glanced down at her number. She smiled and showed it to me; it was 22. I looked at mine and showed it to her. It was the number 11. We both laughed out loud. This may seem magical or supernatural; however, *there is no such thing as super-natural*. There are only *natural things* that are not yet a part of our daily awareness.

This principle is quite simple and one that you may have experienced yourself. For example, have you ever bought a new or used car? After you had narrowed down your selection to a specific make and model of automobile and made your purchase, you probably found that you had spent a considerable amount of time thinking about cars, and in particular that car.

For the next few days, or even weeks after that, didn't it seem like you saw a car like that on every street and highway? The reason lies in your awareness of the car. You established a new program in your inner guidance system with an image of that automobile on it which drew your attention to other cars like it. *Like attracts like*.

Your Inner Guide can use any code symbol *you give to it* and attach *any meaning to it you designate*. This allows you to set up your own personal language with your Inner Guide. As I illustrated earlier, I use it as a quick means to verify something I want an answer to. This is not limited to an insight I need clarified; it could be a yes or no answer to any question or any number of meanings I may wish to use. It could be as simple as choosing what to eat on a menu. Sometimes before I open the menu in a restaurant I might feel like letting my Inner Guide choose what my body needs at the moment. Then I open the menu. Often, I will immediately see an item that has a price of $11 or $22 which tells me that the item is worth considering for the health of my body, since these are my code numbers.

Thus, *I initiate the communication* with my Inner Guide *and it responds* accordingly. An eagle, a Star of David, and certain gemstones, such as jade, amethyst or turquoise, are also code symbols that my Inner Guide and I use to communicate. I encourage you to try this yourself. It's easy to do and fun to make up code symbols that will very soon provide you with ample proof that your Inner Guide is a very real and loving ally working to draw you closer to more abundance in your life.

When you begin, choose something that you very much like and identify what meaning you want your Inner Guide to attach to it. For instance, you may want to start with something very simple to verify *a yes or no significance*. Then, when you see, hear, taste, smell, feel or think about the symbol, you will know right away what it means. Once you become satisfied this is working, other code symbols may be chosen and new meanings applied to them.

Conduits

Conduits are much like code symbols but more elaborate. *A conduit is a bridge* used by many psychics or intuitives to receive inner guidance through pre-structured symbols or direction, but you don't have to be a *practising* psychic or intuitive to use any one of them. *All of us are psychic or intuitive* and any time we are in communication with our Inner Guide we are tuned into that natural ability.

A few of the more common conduits include: Celtic runes, little stones with carved symbols on them, angel cards with single words on them, shaman power decks, cards with symbols or animals on them together with specific interpretations, I Ching coins with meanings connected to them, and many other bridges that create a channel or focus through which our Inner Guide can send direction.

Making your own conduit also allows you to stretch your creative abilities. It's definitely worth the effort because your own personal imprint or vibration is in anything you create and your ability to tune in to information increases as a result.

All of the procedures I have mentioned are conductors **stepping down** the direction given by the Inner Guide which comes from a higher, more subtle vibration to your conscious mind. This provides a symbol through which to interpret your answer. In the case of meditation, symbols are often replaced by visions, much like a movie. In those cases, much of what you receive is complete, like seeing the entire show in a single picture.

I use these systems to **consciously ask for direction** from my Inner Guide rather than waiting for spontaneous direction to just come to me. This creates a **definite link** between me and my Inner Guide clearly tuning into its channel.

Even if you have never tuned into your Inner Guide before, **you have** asked it for advice frequently without knowing. When you say something like, "I wonder what this or that means," in the majority of cases, the answers you received were either missed completely because you didn't think anyone was listening to you, or because you didn't realize your Inner Guide would answer **all** your questions if you **didn't hang up the phone**.

Before I began working with my Inner Guide, on those rare occasions when I did notice an answer, I used to think it was *a coincidence*. I might have thought, "I wonder what so-in-so is doing," only to hear the phone ring and find the person on the other end of the line. In most of those cases it was my Inner Guide that prompted the question in my mind to begin with, since the person on the other end of the phone was likely already thinking about calling me and my link with him stimulated the question in my mind.

If a sincere passion or unselfish emotional appeal is present, as in the example of the mother driving her children home in a thunderstorm, the answer or spontaneous answer-reaction is rarely missed. When I say *rarely missed*, I do not mean it necessarily registers at a conscious level. Even with such a dramatic response, the conscious mind may not connect the Inner Guide to the life-saving reaction. Again, this is usually the case with people who are either unaware of the existence of their Inner Guide or connect little importance to it in their lives.

Interpreting the Symbols

One of my earliest mentors once told me, *"There are many roads to the city of Light."* This means that there are many philosophies, religions and training systems that lead us to our true estate, that awaken us to our Oneness with the 'All that Is,' the all pervasive universe of abundant potential that exists all around and within us—Spirit, God, or whatever name feels most comfortable to us.

Our Inner Guide is *not only a conduit* or personal channel representing one of these roads, but also *a divine aspect* of the 'All that Is' and an aspect of ourselves at the same time. It is a **branch on the vine** of the 'All that Is' and **the heart of that vine is Love.**

There are many roads to the city of light or **awareness** and many ways in which our Inner Guide communicates with us so that we are most able to interpret what is suggested to us. As we open to the wisdom of this marvelous ally, we will discover the ways and means that are most comfortable for us. Many symbols I receive at first appear to make absolutely no sense at all. Sometimes I have to peel away several layers of meaning before I get a sense of the real message hidden within. Nighttime dreams and readings are filled with these types of symbols. This may sound like a tedious job, but it can actually be a lot of fun.

Dream Symbols

Initially, I thought the characters in my dreams represented the actual people they portrayed. But over time, I realized I could rarely make sense of the images and stories using that approach. I soon learned that most of my dreams fell into three categories. **The first** and least common was **an actual vision** of an event yet to come or in the past. In those cases the characters were usually who they represented.

The second dream category was always related to recent events and often re-enacted them in much the same way they had occurred. These dreams, I found, were **a safety valve** for emotional tension releasing the build up during sleep and helping to allow the body to regenerate itself.

But by far **the most common dream** I had and still have occurred when I started working seriously with my Inner Guide. These dreams are either **specific answers** to questions on my mind at the time, or information the Inner Guide sees as important to me.

An interesting thing about these types of dreams is the characters in them. Usually, most of the characters are **aspects of oneself**. For instance, who do you know that reminds you of selfishness? That person would likely show up in your dream as **the selfish part of your ego.**

Go on to think of predominant characteristics in people you know or know about. Who represents power, arrogance, humility, impatience, compassion, persistence, depression, etc.? Can you see the possibilities here? Working with your Inner Guide is always accompanied by **work on yourself**. If your Inner Guide sees an opportunity to show you personal weaknesses that are roadblocks to experiencing a more abundant life, or untapped potential within your character that could increase your experience of abundance, this third dream category is a method it frequently uses.

I became very enthusiastic about working with my Inner Guide when I began experimenting with these dreams. And I soon discovered another very interesting thing about these dreams. I could **ask for them**. That's right. Ask for them, just like ordering from a menu at a restaurant.

Let's say you are having trouble making a decision about taking a promotion in your company that requires you to move to another city immediately. The actual move is not the problem. What concerns you involves an excellent job opportunity you have been looking at in town which, if you leave now, you may miss out on.

You are confused about whether you should take the promotion or pass it up for the other opportunity that you may not even get. Let's say the new opportunity is a stretch for you and requires that you quickly develop new leadership skills. You decide, if you are confident that you have it in you to make this stretch, you will let the promotion go and try for the better job.

Your question to your Inner Guide might be, "Show me in my dreams tonight whether I have the ability to succeed at this new opportunity."

You would go on to **give yourself the command** that **you will** in fact dream tonight, that you will **remember** the dream, and that you will **understand** its meaning.

We are all co-creators with the 'All that Is' and we create all the time, either by intention or by default. When I became aware of this truth it made sense to me to create conditions that were conducive to experiencing more abundance in my life. Now, here's the fun part!

Let's look at a possible dream you may have received in answer to your question. *You observe a teenager standing on the edge of a cliff with a hang glider strapped to his back. He nervously looks over the cliff, takes a deep breath, grits his teeth and jumps off. At first his flight is a little shaky, but soon he begins to soar effortlessly. As he flies comfortably down the slope of the mountain, you notice he has aged and is now a man.* The dream ends and immediately you wake up.

By the way, waking up right after an important dream is very common when you consciously work with your Inner Guide. This ensures you have the best chance of remembering the dream. As always, have a piece of paper and pen beside your bed and jot the dream down right away; then leave it until the next day to interpret. If you have an urge to interpret the dream right away, by all means do so. I find I do better when I am fresh in the morning, but as in all things, it is best to follow your own Inner Guide.

Have you thought of what the dream answer may mean? *Perhaps you figured out your level of ability to handle the new job is represented by the teenager, and his nervousness about the jump is your concern about being able to handle the new opportunity. In the dream, your Inner Guide is telling you to take the new opportunity, which will be a little shaky at the beginning, but will soon feel comfortable as you grow into maturity with the demands of the position.*

When you have worked with your Inner Guide for a while, you will interpret your dreams, readings, page leafings, meditations, conduits, insights, hunches, intuitions and all directions given to you just as easily as that. And you will follow its wise guidance just as quickly.

Inner Guidance Interprets Its Own Symbols

When I first began interpreting my Inner Guide's symbols, I would receive a symbolic suggestion from it, then go on to ask my Inner Guide what the symbol meant. This became a pleasurable exercise, like doing crossword puzzles. The difference is *your Inner Guide helps you* with the words after it gives you the puzzle.

Even today I will get an impression of something I should pay attention to, and because I am not clear on that particular guidance, I will open the first book I see and leaf through it for a confirming word or passage. If I am driving, I might get an urge to turn my head and look at a billboard or a sign in front of a store that has a word or phrase on it that clarifies the insight I just received.

I've even found that by flipping channels on my stereo, a song will have lyrics that explain a symbol, perhaps from a dream I had the night before. You see, *there is no hard and fast rule* of how to interpret the guidance you receive. *The more open you are* to your Inner Guide, the easier it will be to interpret insights you get. Your Inner Guide will use new symbols as clues to interpret symbols it has given to you until, finally, you understand the meaning of the original message, just like the example of the fellow selling a stock that was about to crash.

Your Inner Guide uses the programs within your inner guidance system *to find symbols you will understand*. Try to get into the habit of looking at the symbols given to you *reflected in the mirror of your own character* and circumstances occurring in your life right now. What might they mean to you, specifically? Again, that's why general explanations of symbol meanings are inadequate and may be misleading.

The symbols you receive will often relate to specific subjects that are currently troubling you or that have special interest— particularly, if you are consciously working with your Inner Guide and have asked it for help.

For instance, if you were running naked through a crowd searching for shelter in a night-time dream, this startling symbol may immediately bring to mind a business partnership you were negotiating. It could suggest to you that you were *exposing* your position excessively and need to *cover* yourself better in order to obtain a fair deal.

The actual interpretation comes from the same source as the dream or symbol you received—your Inner Guide. If you are working with your Inner Guide consciously such a quick revelation of the meaning is very common. When the channel between you and your Inner Guide is fine-tuned through constant and conscious communication linked with faith, the direction comes swiftly and is usually very simple to understand.

However, when you first begin to work with your Inner Guide a little digging will be required. The same dream could have *several layers of symbols* which increasingly clarify the meaning to you, much like hydro power needs to be stepped down from its source before electricity can be safely used in your home.

Here is another possible interpretation of the same dream.

Running naked through a crowd may at first suggest a sense of poor self-esteem indicated by the judgmental eyes you feel staring at you. If you have a large ego that explanation may seem incorrect, so you dig a little deeper. You ask your Inner Guide if your first hunch was correct, and if the symbol does represent a poor self-esteem, how does that relate to your large ego?

In this second possible interpretation, you may have begun to search for a deeper meaning to your life, and initially a sense of guilt may be represented by inadequacies you feel within yourself. In this case, your ego shields are being exposed at a deep level and you are beginning to feel uncomfortable at what you see.

After I began working on the inner planes, *I soon discovered my ego was an illusion*. I learned it is directly linked to our inner guidance system and puts up barriers, which I call *ego shields*, attempting to hide the lie of its existence and the truth of our Oneness with the 'All that Is.' The ego has done this very effectively for eons. I soon found out *it was not easily persuaded to give up its hold* over my mind, either.

Your Inner Guide is linked directly to the 'All that Is' and works relentlessly to help you awaken to the abundance that lies within you—all the *faster when you cooperate* with it. The key to quickly understanding what the Inner Guide is suggesting to you is to *cooperate* with it and *have faith* in what it is telling you.

How you interpret the messages from your Inner Guide is a very personal and intimate thing, and although qualified outside assistance can be of value, I suggest you ask your Inner Guide to help you interpret the suggestions *it has given you*. In that way, you will find the answers more quickly because you will be constantly exercising and fine-tuning the channel connecting you to it.

6
BLOCKS TO PURITY— "EGO SHIELDS"

What Illusions Do You Sustain?

Trouble developing an intimate relationship with your Inner Guide is due to blocks in the flow of its direction caused by programs in your inner guidance system.

Your **attention or mental focus is a channel** through which your **energy or life force flows**. Have you ever felt the power of someone's eyes focused on you? I'm sure you have. Even if you were facing in the opposite direction, the force was probably strong enough to make you turn around.

To illustrate that this power is consistent and not haphazard, try taking the opposite position with a little exercise I'm going to suggest. Pick a person sitting alone a short distance from you and stare at that person intently for a minute or two. In this simple exercise, before you begin, you are looking for a person whose thoughts are not too distracted. Think of nothing else, and in your mind's eye see the person turn to look for the source of the inner distraction.

I don't want you throwing this book at me the first chance you get because someone reported you for stalking, so you may want to try this exercise on someone you know so that you can explain yourself afterwards. But don't let the person know what you are doing ahead of time. That may taint the results.

If you try this a few times, I believe you will be convinced *your mind*, right now, has **the power to attract the attention** of other minds that are not focused on anything in particular. With practice, you could attract the attention of any mind. If that is true, how much more do your thoughts *influence your own mind* and its future thoughts?

In most people, the programs in their ego or inner guidance system are the channels through which their attention flows. Like water flowing through a channel, the greater the volume and force of that water, the wider and deeper it becomes. The channel becomes a stream, the stream becomes a river and, occasionally, the river overflows its banks causing destruction through flooding.

Consider what channels now exist in your ego or inner guidance system. They will tell you what you are giving your attention to. By consistently giving your attention to something, *you give it your power* and that *sustains its life.*

Because **the ego is an illusion,** it can only direct you *to create other illusions*. The channels within its programs are therefore illusions that are **kept alive** by the power of your focused attention. Anything which emanates from an illusion is *temporary*, no matter how long its life may be. Therefore, in order to recognize the fruits of the ego, **look for those things which are not permanent**

Things which are **permanent** emanate or extend from the 'All that Is' and anything that is One with the 'All that Is' is *eternal*. True abundance is eternal while material abundance by itself is temporary. But because we live in a material world as well as a spiritual world, to live with true abundance requires the temporary material abundance as well. However, material abundance is a term relative to your individual life. Some people *need* more materiality to fulfill their destiny, while others need very little.

To live abundantly in the material world of illusions requires an understanding of *who is the master and who is the servant*. This is the meaning of the old adage *to live in the world but not of the world.* It means that we *recognize* the need for abundance in the material world as a tool or servant of our will and destiny and not a master of it.

It is our *attachment* to material abundance and *our belief in limitation* that brings on a feeling of lack and makes us a servant to it. If a person is detached from material abundance, their attention will dwell on it only to the extent of their true needs and no more. Attachment to anything temporary is a channel for the ego.

This is why a channel linking you and your Inner Guide based on trust is vital to the experience of true abundance, which you will recall is *a balanced life, wanting for nothing, filled with Peace, Love and Joy.*

If your attention is focused on the guiding light of your Inner Guide, an abundant life is what it will direct you to. And in the process the rivers, streams and channels used by the ego *will dry up* as you *reroute your focus* only to those things which are permanent. In this way your Inner Guide will lead you back to the eternal which will reawaken you to your Oneness with the 'All that Is.'

The Ego

Our ego is an illusion! Now that's a heavy statement isn't it? We defend ourselves with the power of our ego's sense of righteous indignation, judgment and superiority from egotistical conduct in others. Is that a paradox or what? It's a classic example of fighting fire with fire.

Do you know what we get when we fight fire with fire? More fire! We need to fight fire with water. However, metaphorically the ego thrives on fire, and in this case *fire represents chaos*. Peace, tolerance, compassion, forgiveness and all other branches of love, are water to the ego's fire and cannot long be permitted to exist in our consciousness if it is to survive.

But how can we live without our ego? It's our *identity*, isn't it? A consciousness of guilt, fear, chaos and limitation is the offspring of our ego no matter what *band aid attitude* we may use to hide its control of our true abundant estate.

This is an identity *unworthy* of *the greatness that lies within* us. Our discovery of or even our suspicion that this is true is a serious threat to the ego that clings to its temporary hold over us with the tenacity and ferocity of a wounded animal.

When we first begin the work of linking with, listening to and obeying the direction of our Inner Guide, *the assault mounted by our ego can be enormous*. All manner of subterfuge will be used to sway us from this deadly course. When the knowingness of our Oneness with the 'All that Is' hits us, when the AHA experience of this *Truth* gently touches our minds with its ecstatic revelation, the death dirge begins to play for our ego.

It senses this and cannot tolerate it. A battle ensues and like the warrior Arjuna in *The Bagavad Gita*, we soon realize the enemy lies within. It is an exciting period in our awakening as the layers of darkness are peeled away from our inner eye and we gradually see **the tiny prison of limitation** we have allowed ourselves to dwell within. But **we hold the key** and have always held it and it is our Inner Guide who will gently lead us through the battle with our ego to the summit of our true identity, conscious awareness of our Oneness with the 'All that Is.'

We must not think we lose our individuality, for that is the first weapon of falsehood in the ego's defense system. Its serpent's tongue will weave many **logical tales**, but they are all lies. Lay all doubts, confusion and seeming contradictions on the footstool of your Inner Guide and the fog will soon disperse.

When once we awaken to our true estate, we realize we are a conscious living **individual** entity inextricably One with all other units of individuality working in perfect synchronous harmony. What a way to live: **All for one and one for all!** United we stand tall. **This is humankind's destiny**.

Below I have listed a few of the common soldiers in the ego's army. All are obstacles to our link with our Inner Guide and our eventual awakening.

Ego Shields

As I have discussed, energy must flow for its creative power to be expressed. I also illustrated that a desired outcome must have a **focus** in order to guide the necessary energy, thereby attracting suitable conditions for the goal to come into being. **Energy therefore follows thought**. Any block to the consistent flow of energy reduces or curtails the manifestation of the desired result.

Ego shields are blocks the ego creates to protect itself from real or imagined threats. They were formed in part due to painful experiences endured by the ego in the past. Over time, the shield becomes more or less insulated according to our exposure to similar experiences. In some cases it disappears altogether and, in others, it becomes a veritable fortress attempting to shield the ego from the slightest repetition of the offending experience.

The obvious drawback to an ego shield is that it works both ways. That is to say, any good that might have come to you from similar experiences is blocked reducing your exposure to much joy and abundance.

For example, a ***defensive attitude*** is an ego shield that can quickly alienate a potentially healthy and joyful relationship before it has a chance to get started. This is as true for a man or woman suspicious of the motives of a new suitor as it is of a country hesitant to establish ties with another country through an inordinate fear of loss. This shield should not be confused with healthy pragmatism.

Here are some examples of some of the most common ***ego shields***:

Spite (anger, hatred, revenge, malevolence)

A thinking process that illustrates this ego shield includes, "I'll show them. I'll never let that happen to me again as long as I live." A severe attack of any kind leaving deep unhealed scares helps to create this shield. It can be a formidable motivation for achievement ***at any price*** and often leads to an attitude of "look out for number one," "dog eat dog," "survival of the fittest," and "every man/woman for themselves."

Defensiveness (excessive caution, timidity, introversion)

Typical comments heard from an inner guidance system programmed with this shield include, "What do you mean by that comment?" "It's not my fault!" and "I can't help it!" **Poor self esteem** is usually behind this shield. It also has elements of fear of failure.

Cynicism (scoffing, ridicule, sarcasm, belittling)

This shield inspires comments like, "Forget about it, no government is ever going to balance the budget," "If I had a dollar for every lie I ever heard I'd be a millionaire long ago." This ego shield is connected to a lack of trust in yourself as well as poor self esteem. In order for the inner guidance system to protect the ego from sliding into further insignificance, everything and everyone must be **put down**, below the current status of the ego. This twisted reasoning makes it possible for the ego to survive without descending into a constant state of depression.

Aggressiveness (warlikeness, cruelty, brutality)

This ego shield occurs in many places and can frequently be found in situations where a **false belief in limitation** or a **deep seated insecurity** is prevalent . For example: "There is not enough land or food to go around. We must protect what is ours and take what is not ours if need be." Or, "There are just so many management positions and one of them has got my name on it." This is a **'larger than life,' 'in-your-face'** ego shield and has an attitude that **force** is the only way to get where it wants to go and when the destination is reached it represents some form of security. It is also a powerful ego shield seen in over achievers who feel they must **be in control** to be secure.

In its more acceptable social form, it is almost considered an attribute. "The sky is the limit," "shoot for the stars," and "anything is possible" describe the attractive cloak around this shield that makes it appear benign. In good times the less desirable "survival of the fittest" aspect that characterizes this shield is hidden, but when times get lean, the teeth quickly grow long and sharp. A ***constant sense of urgency*** together with a ***simmering anxiety*** accompanies this shield and illustrates a deep fear of loss.

Arrogance (conceit, condescension, smugness)

One of the more distasteful and alienating ego shields is arrogance. It tends to have the exact opposite effect on those it most wants to influence. Born of a weak self esteem, it displays itself as anything but weak. For example, "Just give me the job and I'll run it up the flagpole," or "there isn't much I haven't seen or done, so don't try to tell me the way it is."

An interesting paradoxical effect for the one who uses this shield frequently is the ***disdain*** it generates for anyone gullible enough to be impressed by its bluff. The ego knows the shield is bogus and loses respect for those that believe in it. It wants to impress those that don't believe it and so becomes ***obsequious, groveling*** to those who are not impressed. Both attitudes are painful as are all the fruits of all the ego's actions.

Intimidation (belligerence, threats, manipulation)

Examples of this ego shield include, "Well if you can't help me then I guess I'll just have to get the manager!" "Do I have to do everything myself? Can't you do anything right?"

This is also an ***in-your-face*** ego shield, but rarely has any substance behind its threats. It usually has more ***bluff and bluster*** about it than real significance. The deeply insecure surround themselves with this shield and often *appear aloof* and *superior*, which is the opposite of the truth.

Judgement (criticism, scorn, strong opinions)

There may not be an ego shield more prevalent than this one. Hardly a minute goes by that we are not making some sort of judgement on something or somebody. Common examples may include, "I can't stand people who do that all the time," or "I don't know what she sees in him. I wouldn't have a person who thinks that way in my own home."

While the judgement associated with decision making is essential to our day to day life, when once we *let go* completely and allow the Inner Guide to direct our life, all decisions are *instantaneous* and *perfect* for us in the moment.

There is about this particular ego shield a very interesting and valuable point when viewed through the eyes of the Inner Guide's direction. The ego primarily uses judgement as *a shield against self discovery*. Looking inward at our obstacles to growth would eventually reveal the truth *that the ego is an illusion*. Therefore, the ego makes this a painful search and allows us to escape this suffering by easily recognizing the very things that upset us the most in ourselves by seeing their *reflection in other people*.

This is why *the people who upset us the most are our best teachers*. If we will allow ourselves to see them that way, the rate of our growth will increase dramatically.

Some of the most prevalent causes behind the creation of ego shields are as follows:

Repeated failure leads to "fear of failure"

Repeated loss leads to "fear of loss and insecurity"

Betrayal leads to "lack of trust"

Guilt leads to "lack of self love, worthiness and self trust"

Lack of love and nurturing leads to "lack of self worth, need for attention and a feeling of being separated from everyone and everything else"

Despite the powerful motivating force behind many ego shields, their achievements are little more than superficial since their use always lacks a flow of joyful and abundant feelings. What joy is there when we withhold love and kindness, and replace it with criticism, manipulation and hatred for others? How does burying our gifts create more? We use them or lose them!

The Power of "They Say" to Control Our Habits

Think of *"They"* as a facet of mankind's group consciousness. Not long ago a movie came out called *Men in Black*. The organization behind the men in black explained that in fact *they were "They."* I found it humorous that when the clandestine "They" finally began to emerge from the shadows, the first thing we saw was a manipulative group of 'privileged and informed, high-tech, spy-like, cartoon characters dressed in black with questionably, benign motives.'

The description hit the nail on the head. "They" were recruited from those of the general population who displayed some particular expertise or value to "They's" purpose.

But the bottom line is *"we are they,"* and we are just discovering it now. Most of us have always suspected as much but never gave it a lot of thought. The reason is clear: It just didn't seem that important.

The subject can be irritating when we identify "They" with trendsetters who control our lives and set up barriers that appear impossible to surmount. "They get you coming and going, don't they?" "They'll do it to you every time!" "They say it's impossible to do that!" Conversely, "They" may seem all knowing, setting trend-creating standards for how we should live, think and act. "They say 'this or that' music is *really in* now' ", or "they say everyone will be wearing that fashion in the spring."

Where Does It All Start?

The root of a trend that becomes a "they say" statement imbedded into mankind's group consciousness of reality is, at least for the moment, what I call a *power burst*. The power burst can be the onslaught of a pet rock phenomena, mini skirts, small cars or big trucks, personal computers, the Internet or cellphones.

It is usually in response to a significant and underlying need felt by a large segment of the population. The trend answers the need on a superficial level and provides a temporary band aid cure, dulling whatever discomfort that exists beneath the surface. It can be a localized phenomena or it can blanket the world.

Before the trend, fad or phenomena is recognized as part of our daily life, it begins as a frequently heard "they say." When put into the spin cycle of the "they say" machine, the grapevine technology and merchandisers swiftly launch the new ideology *from potential to accepted reality*.

Power burst suggests a source of energy sufficient to ignite something, like a blasting cap used to set off dynamite. Its size may seem insignificant, but it packs a sufficient wallop to start a trend.

The source is thought, focused thought that comes from deep inside. Usually a single source to begin with, but quickly fired into a flame by like-minded people.

An unshakable belief in something followed by a burning desire to see the idea manifest into reality provides the conduit for the "they say" machine to crank up. Sustained focus of this burning desire is all that is required to see it through to fruition.

It needs concerted **action**, but no one could describe it as either difficult or hard work. In fact, the work may appear almost effortless to one whose desire is fueled by a deep abiding faith that *sees* the successful completion long before it comes into being. *The scope and lifetime of the new "They say" trend is in direct proportion to the relief it offers the specific discomfort existing in the world at the time.*

The Followers Line Up

The dynamo throws off an almost invincible magnetic pulse that *attracts* followers and supporters from far and wide. Many, having no particular direction of their own, are swept into the growing flood of followers chanting the slogans of "they say."

The "they say" machine consists mainly of followers who support the growing force and *mindlessly add their life force* to it. They are like drones fanning the flames and stoking the fires, but are not part of the original fire themselves. This is only one step away from *the mob instinct* we see in riot and panic situations.

Giving Away Our Power

Whether the emerging power is a Third Reich, a fashion trend or a fitness craze, unconscious union with the power flow is **power given away**, and when we give away our power, **we are prisoners to someone else's direction**.

Control, or rather **being controlled**, is the result, usually at an unconscious level. The **sacrifice of our decision making power**—and in its most insidious case, our **personal freedom** to choose—is **the price we pay** for acquiescing to the suggestions of "they say." The size and comfort of the cage may be such that we do not even see the bars. They are there all the same—**robbing our free will** and subjecting us to a road whose direction and end we can only guess.

Real Power

Real power is the vitality that energizes the things **you want** to create or animates the things you have already created that have been motivated by your **heart's desire, your destiny**. Without it, your fondest dreams and most passionate desires go by the wayside.

It is **not influenced or colored** by the ego's shields or by **what 'they say'** you should think, say or do. It flows **unrestricted** from your mind and is **guided by love** which always influences the direction given to you by your Inner Guide. Its motives are **always pure** and oriented to **the good of All**. It cannot be **bought** at any price, for it would then immediately lose its power. This is because all creations extended from the 'All that Is' are permanent, while all created by the ego are temporary, having no real life or existence.

Real power is power that is *given away in the service of others*. It is not ours to keep, but it is ours *to use*. In the truest sense, when we work in harmony with our Inner Guide, we are following *the will* of the 'All that Is.' In our capacity as co-creators with the 'All that Is,' *we act as conduits* for Its power to flow through to other parts of Itself, which includes us. The more we *yield* to this power and allow it to flow through us uninterrupted by ego issues, the larger our capacity becomes to accept and use Its power to create.

Thus the ancient saying:

> *To those who have been given much, much is expected.*

Real power is the only power there is since it flows from the 'All that Is.' *All else is an illusion of power,* no matter how real it may temporarily appear.

Power Must Flow Unrestricted

If our body is to function in a healthy, vibrant fashion, we must have a constant flow of energy. If we cut off that flow, for instance, by practising poor nutrition or a destructive lifestyle, the automatic rebuilding and regenerating of our cells slows down. The result? Illness, debility, rapid aging, lack of well being, and death.

For example, if a company is to survive, energy in the form of capital must flow through its veins. Without product sales and healthy management of the funds that flow from them, the corporation becomes weak, unable to support its employees and expand.

A nation's health also emanates from a healthy flow of energy called power. If the balance of that power is disturbed, for example, through greed, the ripple effect touches lives everywhere and eventually creates dissension leading to government collapse.

Energy Constipation

Virtually everyone has at one time or another experienced this uncomfortable physical condition arising from a block in the natural elimination process. Even a few hours or this unpleasant adventure begins to back up the entire well being of the body. Two or three days of it can begin lead to serious side effects requiring medical attention. Left unchecked, the body dies.

All power in the form of energy must circulate unimpeded for the health of its host to continue.

'Attachment' Blocks the Flow of Energy

If we are **attached** to something, we fear losing it. "If you let it go it will return," or "If you want to keep him, set him free." These quotations exemplify the lyrics from a typical country song, nevertheless they have profound significance and truth to them.

What we hold onto, controls us. "Wow! That's heavy," you may say. "You mean if I love my job, it controls me?" No, not if the love is without strings. What I mean is this: If you cannot see yourself living joyfully without the job, for any reason, it controls you and what controls you imprisons you. *Lack of freedom is not joyful.*

Take a moment now and list three reasons why you love your job (if you do):

1. _____

2. _____

3. _____

Now, which is the most important point you have listed?

How would you feel if either the job or the reason you enjoy it were taken away from you right now? Would you feel abandoned, insecure, sick to your stomach, anxious, angry or all of the above?

"Hey!" you say, "It's only natural to feel like that when you lose something really important to you." **Common** yes, but *natural* no! Any of the negative feelings above are common because most people would feel the same way. But those feelings are not joyful nor abundant and my objective in this book is to help you find a more joyful and abundant life. Therefore, anything which is *unlike joy or abundance must be exposed and identified* before its opposite condition can be found.

Once again, it is the process of *not this, not that*, that will help you to determine *what* it is that leads to *a true state of abundance* in your life. To help you with this *self discovery*, make a list of *ALL* the people, places, things and circumstances you are now attached to, leaving *nothing out*. This will require *total honesty* on your part, but the result will show where many of the obstacles to true abundance in your life lie.

Things I am attached to:

1. _____

2. _____

3. _____

4. _____

5. _____

6. _____

7. _____

8. _____

9. _____

10. _____

11. _____

12. _____

13. _____

14. _____

15. _____

16. _____

17. _____

18. _____

19. _____

20. _____

If you need to, continue your list at the end of this book so that it will be easy to locate when you work on the next step, *letting go*.

Letting Go

Attachment to anything, whether it is a person, place, thing or circumstance, is due to a **belief in limitation**. It promotes a **consciousness of poverty** and a **fear of loss** when compared to the true abundance that lies within waiting to come into your life.

In the real world that lies within us all, there is **no limitation or lack** and it is through our Inner Guide that we will be led back to that wonderful state of awareness. Once we begin to realize that all things that lead to true abundance **already exist** within us, the next step in **letting go** is allowing it to **flow** from you by **extending it to all** knowing there is an **inexhaustible supply** for everyone.

Notice I said **extend** it not **project** it. Projecting is a term often used by proponents of The Fish Story—Part Two. It is a term that **believes** a **state of separation** exists in the world. **Extension** confirms that **you know All is One** in the universe and therefore **you** must be part of it. How can you **project** anything **out of** a state of Oneness? You can only extend yourself to another part of yourself.

Granted, this may be a little difficult to get your mind around at first. Therefore, I suggest you imagine a circle representing the 'All that Is' and a pinpoint within it representing your individual identity. For you to **create** something permanent, you must extend a portion of the **'All that Is'** that you are a part of, to another portion of **It**. If you have extended your creations, they must still be a part of you and cannot be lost.

Through your **power of thought**, extension of the 'All that Is' is possible, provided it includes **'ALL.'** This is why **selflessness** is essential in **the attraction** of true abundance into your life. For truly, if you are serving 'ALL,' **you must be serving** *yourself.* Where is the *fear of loss*, the *fear of letting go* in that scenario?

Letting go of attachments *does not mean abandoning anything* that is in harmony with true abundance. It means having an attitude of *release* from being a slave to that which we are attached to. It means we are *the master not the servant* to the creations we have extended from ourselves.

Neither possessing great wealth or living from paycheck to paycheck indicates true abundance or the lack of it. Rather, it is your attitude of attachment or lack of it to your material situation that determines your freedom or bondage to it. And remember, *freedom* is a prerequisite to living a truly abundant life.

Letting go is not a theoretical concept that cannot be taken seriously when viewed from a material standpoint. The proof lies in the fear of loss associated with attachments of any kind. The *consequences of fear of loss* are not limited to mere anxiousness and other related uncomfortable feelings. It also extends to the creation of the conditions *we do not want*, that being *actual loss*.

Truly has it been said, *"Our worst fears come upon us."* The reason is simple in light of our power to create through our thoughts. The things we are most attached to *we fear losing the most*. That means we give the most thought energy to those things we fear losing, *attracting the very conditions* to bring about their *certain loss*.

Letting go also allows us to *release* those things that are not in harmony with abundance. Although, when we are attached to them, they may not appear that way.

BUILDING BRIDGES OVER BLOCKS

Worthiness, the Door to Receiving True Abundance

Worthiness is an aspect of *Self Love* and the *antithesis of guilt*. To love one's Self means that we must rise above guilt. *The antidote is forgiveness.*

Of all the blocks to true abundance, a lack of Self Worth or Self Esteem, due to guilt, is the greatest. If we believe we do not deserve *we will not open ourselves to receive*. Because it is too painful to accept that we do not deserve, instead of forgiving ourselves, the ego creates a shield or series of shields *to camouflage* the real cause of lack in our lives.

Once we awaken to our Oneness with the 'All that Is,' we realize that it is impossible to be guilty of anything. We were merely reacting to mistakes made in the illusionary world of temporary things. And if they were illusionary, *the guilt could not be real either* and forgiveness is instantaneous.

Until we attain that lofty consciousness, that realization is beyond our awareness and guilt and its offspring, lack of self worth, continues. But any habit programmed into our inner guidance system can be broken and new habits can be created.

Breaking Old Habits and Creating New Ones

Ego shields are habits anchored in the inner guidance system. To eliminate any habit *we must rise above it*, giving it *no thought* or *energy* through our focused attention. But how do you stop thinking about something when it is a habit. Habits tend to be right in front of your nose, don't they?

The answer is to focus your attention **on the opposite condition**. For example, if you want to stop smoking, you don't say to yourself with a strong resolve, "I will never smoke again!" That will simply give the thought/habit more energy/life and make you want to smoke more. Instead, you would say, "I *now* have perfectly healthy lungs!"

That statement, strictly speaking, is not true, since if you smoke, it would be impossible to have perfectly healthy lungs *now*. But the body's health follows the **direction of your thoughts** and time is meaningless in the realm of thought. With sufficient faith, that perfectly healthy condition would manifest immediately. But even without a sufficient faith to create the desired condition immediately, by sticking to this new focused attention, the inner guidance system will soon contain a new program called "perfectly healthy lungs."

Because thoughts are **magnetic** and **attract** the conditions that are conducive to their manifestation, not only would you soon stop smoking but you would also attract many other conditions into your life that further promoted perfectly healthy lungs. For example, you may be attracted to more foods that contain antioxidants or you may develop a strong desire to begin a daily walking routine.

What you have done, in effect, is to **withdraw energy from the old habit** and **redirect it to the new habit**. Without energy guided by your thoughts, the ego shield will wither and die. When we **switch our attention** and the energy that flows behind it to the new program, it is established in our inner guidance system as **a positive tool** that can be used by your Inner Guide to help awaken you to your true estate—Oneness with the "All that Is." Naturally, this depends on wisely choosing a new program that will be correct for you. And this will happen if you allow yourself to be piloted by your **Inner Guide**.

By the way, I am not calling the smoking habit an ego shield, but it is evidence of the self destructive tendencies evolving out of all ego shields.

The Power of "Icons"

What does an icon mean to you? Icons are symbols like the logo used on company letterhead or positioned strategically at the top of a skyscraper. Some are so obscure they appear to represent nothing at all. But, over time, the character can take on significant symbolic meaning that can depict infinitely more than the tiny graphic illustrates.

I will use this little example to expand on my meaning. When you see the symbol **GM**, what comes to mind? In this case, the symbol is so significant even the mention of the letters can conjure up a wealth of information for most people.

It may remind you of a powerful, international corporation employing millions of people directly or indirectly, and providing quality transportation, enjoyment and security to countless more millions the world over.

These thoughts and many others do not register as such when you see the symbol or icon, rather they stimulate a *feeling* summing up the *essence* of the icon. In your case that essence is unique to you.

For example, your very first car may have been a used GM product, beat up, barely road worthy that rattled and clanked its way down the highway, but you loved every moment you owned it! Years later you may have owned a brand new GM automobile but experienced a continual service problem that just never got fixed to your satisfaction. Later, you found out it was the mechanic's inexperience and not the fault of the car, but the icon took on that irritating memory.

The result is a sweet and sour emotion each time you see the icon. And yet you actually programmed the meaning of the icon into your subconscious mind and allowed those messages to remain connected to the memory. The icon's affect on you was therefore semi-automatic (pun intended). The circumstances creating the sweet and sour experience happened *to you*, but *you allowed them* to remain attached to the icon, either *by choice* or by default *through indifference* since you may not have been aware of the process going on at the time.

Now let's use this icon in a theoretical situation and see how it can be useful to your purpose. Say you are an actor and have to play a scene requiring you to convey a sweet and sour feeling to the audience. By consciously *overlaying* the sweet and sour, mood altering effect of the icon onto your part in the scene, you create the desired result. Whether or not you were unaware of the process behind the creation of the Icon's effect on you does not diminish its usefulness to you in this case.

Aromas from the past are icons as are certain sounds, such as pieces of music. I am certain as you read these words that you can recall a wonderful aroma or a favorite song that immediately attracts a rush of good feelings.

The aroma of grandma's apple pie floating through the house, a love song you and your first sweetheart shared in high school, the roar of an engine reminiscent of your first motorcycle, a perfume worn by the teacher you had a crush on in grade 4— these are typical Icons that float to the surface of our memories. They easily bring with them feelings as strong and wonderful as if it were the first time you experienced them.

But it could just as easily be an unpleasant feeling. In fact there are many icon's buried deep within our subconscious minds that are difficult to pinpoint, but when triggered, dredge up unpleasant memories and bring about negative changes in our attitude. For instance, **many of the prejudices** we adhere to are associated with things that hurt us in the past. We tend to *'paint new experiences with the same brush.'*

As a child, perhaps you were constantly taunted by a bully who happened to be of another race, color or creed than yourself. That memory could have tainted your attitude toward all people of the same background for the rest of your life. Likewise, the stereotype of the 'used car salesman' has made millions of people defensive when going through the experience of buying a car, new or used.

Icons have great power to alter our way of thinking. Armed with that knowledge, *we can use them to rise above the ego shields* programmed into our inner guidance system and replace them with positive programs that are useful to the Inner Guide's ultimate purpose.

We Can Create our Own Icons

We can intentionally create our own private Icons that *stimulate specific moods* and feelings, and positively influence our attitude and attract conditions that lead to greater joy and abundance. Once the icon is *anchored*, the swiftness with which this process works may be compared to the instantaneous activities of a high speed computer.

Let's go ahead and create an example of an icon now.

Begin by listing below five character traits you feel hold you back from experiencing the maximum joy and abundance in your life.

1. _____

2. _____

3. _____

4. _____

5. _____

From this list, choose the one you feel represents the greatest handicap to attracting joy and abundance into your life.

Next, I want you to select a symbol that best represents that character trait. Allow your mind to flow freely when doing this rather than trying to *figure out* a symbol and chose the very first symbol that comes to mind. Your Inner Guide knows the best link to use between the trait and a symbol. Let's say the character trait you chose was *timidness*. A symbol for timidness might call to mind a baby bunny. You would then write the words *baby bunny* beside the *timidness*.

Now let a symbol representing the opposite of a timid baby bunny flow into your mind, say a *lion*.

Now with a lion as your icon, list all the character traits you consider *desirable* about the lion that are the opposite to your timidness. If you feel there are some undesirable characteristics in lions, then simple don't add them to the list.

Then, at the top of the list in bold capital letters write these words:

I NOW MANIFEST THESE LION TRAITS!

You can add or delete points from the list at any time, molding and finetuning the icon you are programming into your inner guidance system.

Anchoring the Icon

The next thing you want to do is **anchor** this icon into your inner guidance system. There are many ways to do this, but I like the simple 3" X 5" card method. You find a picture of a lion that **feels** right for you and best represents the character traits you have listed then paste it at the top of the card. Then you write out the bold statement

I NOW MANIFEST THESE LION TRAITS!

under the picture of the lion. Below you list the points you made from your original list.

Several times every day take out the card, look at the lion and read what you have written, preferably aloud. The more sensory input you use, in this case visual and auditory, the faster the 'lion icon' will anchor into your inner guidance system. Within a very short time, usually a few days, your *'lion icon'* will begin to **overshadow** the traits you symbolized with the baby bunny. And within a week they will begin to dominate the traits you wish to delete.

I recommend continuing for *at least 21 days* to allow the 'lion icon' to completely anchor itself. The final step is to keep the icon *where you can see it often*. This could be in the form of a little sticker placed in the corner of your washroom mirror or in the form magnet centered on your fridge. One of my icons is a beautiful statue of an eagle I've placed on my office desk right above my computer where I see it all the time.

You need not consciously look at the icon after it has become anchored. Your Inner Guide will fix on it behind the scenes and amplify the symbol's power every time It sees it or something like it.

If you have any doubts about the **habit changing power** of icons, have a good look at the names and pictures of animals representing sports clubs. There is a veritable jungle of animals out there on the ball courts and playing fields of the world. The power people behind sports clubs are well aware of the value these Icons hold to stimulate both the players and the fans.

Animals have an easy and obvious symbolism but are not the only representations that work. For example, consider the *swastika*. While most people immediately conjure up uneasy feelings when they see this powerful icon, the swastika originally meaning meant *well being*. That ancient symbol has been widely used throughout history but is best known as the emblem of the Nazi Party. The evil and carnage associated with its recent historical symbolism has completely changed its original meaning.

In other words, the icon was *reprogrammed* by the powerful yet destructive thoughts, words and deeds associated with its recent use. Likewise, you can program any symbol with precisely what works for you, anchor it to your inner guidance system and *use it as a friendly ally* to influence your attitude and attract conditions that are joyful and abundant.

Once anchored, your icons become automatic servants *that attract circumstances, people, ideas and personal growth* which are in harmony with the programming you have given them. It would be prudent, therefore, to always allow yourself to be directed by your Inner Guide in the choice of these power-ful symbols and the programming behind them.

7
Seeking
the Highest Ideal

The School of Life

Imagine yourself sitting down with a wise and kindly mentor as you prepare to enter college. Your objectives might include critical details that range from choosing the right university, entering the correct curriculum relevant to your talents and interests, to more personal details like finding a suitable place to live that is conducive to your greatest degree of happiness and success in school.

One of your primary goals may be to obtain a degree that will help provide you with *a solid foundation* from which to build a happy life, filled with prosperity and fulfillment.

One of the fondest dreams of loving parents is to see this scenario played out to successful fruition for their children. The 'All that Is' has a similar focus and has provided the *school of life* to help us achieve graduation. That is, to awaken us to our Oneness with It and all the *wisdom, love* and *power* that is and has always been available to us when that glorious state of awareness comes upon us.

Think of your Inner Guide as a deeply loving and highly qualified mentor who *knows precisely how to steer you* through the school called life to that awakening. The primary difference in these two scenarios is our awareness or lack of awareness of the wonderful ally we have in our Inner Guide.

Once we accept its reality and, through receptive eyes and ears, learn to trust its loving guidance, the educational process advances at incredible speed and with far more adventure and exhilaration then we may have thought possible.

When we really begin to trust and obey our Inner Guide's suggestions, Its guidance will seem almost magical. As a result, one of the first hurdles we must overcome is the *phenomena* aspect we may be tempted to associate with It.

This natural feeling that we are somehow involved in a supernatural relationship with an unseen entity within us slows the growth of our alliance with It. Why is that? It is because things we find *awesome, phenomenal or unbelievable* do not register with our inner guidance system as normal everyday experiences.

Consequently, they are relegated to the field of *periodic occurrences* at best. In other words, to tell ourselves our Inner Guide is an *unbelievable entity* actually *solidifies our doubt* that it is real. Therefore, a casual while respectful acceptance of this wonderful ally suggests its *normalcy* to our inner guidance system and resistance to a growing closeness with it fades.

As an offshoot of recognizing the normalcy of having an Inner Guide as a mentor, friend and ally, a gradual evaporation of belief in coincidence, chance and luck occurs. We learn there is a *cause* behind every *effect* and while many causes will elude our understanding on our way to awakening, a solid trusting link with our Inner Guide will blanket us with a gentle and peaceful acceptance that the universe is indeed unfolding as it should.

Peace

A sense of *inner peace* is perhaps the greatest underlying benefit of linking with and trusting your Inner Guide. A profound sense of security spills over the waterfall of its essence leaving a *tranquil space* within that clearly reflects all that it has to share with us. This peace also replaces the anxiety associated with crisis and the panic related to deadlines with an urgency guided by calmness. I call this feeling *relaxed intensity*.

Relaxed intensity is a laser-like focus on what is real and true, unruffled by the temporal constraints of time and space. It is a powerful state of *centeredness* that lives in the eye of the storm swirling around us in the material world. It is literally a state of *heaven on earth*.

The Power of Detachment

Possession does not necessarily indicate attachment to something. It can simply mean a state of ownership on a physical level, but not attachment on a mental or emotional level. To the extent that you *must have* something in your life in order to be satisfied, you are in bondage to it.

If the essence of your goal is to experience abundance that is without end, *a balanced life, wanting for nothing, and filled with Peace, Love and Joy*, you must detach yourself from the need to possess anything. You may indeed own many things and wield great power, if that is your destiny, but you cannot be attached to the possessions or the power if you are going to remain free.

Freedom and detachment are synonymous. The opposite of freedom is bondage or slavery and wanting for nothing cannot coexist with slavery to anyone or anything. This is the meaning of the wise proverb, *"Be in the world but not of the world."*

Not long ago I was watching the women's Olympic figure skating championship. The hands down favorite skated a near perfect routine and all the experts were sure she would take the gold medal. Then, a tiny, fifteen-year-old girl skated a dazzling routine that left everyone dumbfounded. She not only captured the gold medal, but also the hearts and minds of everyone who witnessed her magnificent performance.

After the awards ceremony, the young champion and her runner-up sat down together to be interviewed for world television. The pride and bliss on the champion's face was heartwarming, but what really struck me was the *grace after defeat* displayed by the girl favored to win, who had placed second.

She explained how she had three specific goals since childhood. The first was to compete at the Olympics in figure skating. The second was to skate her very best, and the third was to win a gold medal. Quietly, and with deep sincerity and grace, she shared her thankfulness for achieving two of her three goals. Then, with relaxed intensity, she suggested she might try again at the next Olympics.

Her ability to speak with such grace and genuine appreciation despite her second place finish I found more inspiring than her actual skating performance. To achieve the level of perfection required to compete at the Olympic level demanded years of dedication, practice and a passion to excel at the highest level. But behind the achievement was something much more.

Who she had become in the process of pursuing her goals was a shining example of what we all can be if we use the power of *passion* over that of a *burning desire*. She had dedicated herself to being the best she could be as a human being in a specific field of endeavor, and had detached herself from that accomplishment by gifting it to the world for all to share. Had she been attached to her goal, the defeat would have showed as a bitter disappointment on her face and in her words, no matter how hard she may have tried to hide it.

Everyone who witnesses the performance of such an unselfish example of excellence feels a part of the grandeur of it. The *bonding power of Love* for the achievement as well as *from* the achiever acknowledges the Oneness we all share within the 'All that Is.'

In this way, all are lifted a little by the accomplishment and the detached expression of the achiever frees her of the consequences of the results, not only of losing but of winning. She has *given it away* and what came back was the *essence* of her goal. The blissful link with the 'All that Is' and the love-link with all those she shared her achievement.

Detachment is freedom. It is freedom to experience all things without the need for a specific result. And freedom gives us *a feeling of peaceful security*. We cannot be controlled by something that we are not attached to. *We simply experience it*.

Self Reliance

Guidance, no matter what source you chose to follow, can only lead you to *the work you must do on yourself*. And no guidance outside yourself is without flaws. It is influenced by the programs present *within the source* of that guidance.

Imagine a beaker of crystal clear, pure water which represents the *truth of the universe.* Vials of this pure water are given to the world through individuals that have been purified by love and dedicated to the service of others.

Throughout history we have seen the outward manifestation of this *pure liquid light filled water.* We give these manifestations names like Christianity, Buddhism, Hinduism, Judaism, Islam, Taoism, and a host of lesser known beliefs.

The liquid light also appears in soul-inspired artistic endeavor, such as the spirit moving concertos and sonatas of Handel. It stands majestically before us in the pyramids of Egypt and the Sistine Chapel's exquisite frescoes created by Michaelangelo. It can be found in Leonardo da Vinci's painting of The Last Supper and flawlessly sculpted in the statue of David, also by Michaelangelo. We see it in ballet and choreography and even in the symmetry of a marching band.

Mother Earth herself proudly portrays the light of life in her magnificent mountains, her sublime sunsets and radiant rainbows. She rhythmically sways in perfect harmony with the constant movement of life in her oceans and pours this life freely through her veins in a multitude of rivers and streams.

In a million other places, our senses are exposed to the *creative manifestations* of the pure liquid light originating from the beaker of universal truth.

To the individual creators of masterpieces of peace, joy and upliftment, the vial pours out its perfection untainted. But unless experienced from an Inner Guided perspective, the experience is diluted. Experienced, secondhand through the direction of others, the light within the masterpiece must flow through their individual inner guidance programs, their own **rose colored glass**.

Imagine a drop of color merging with the pure liquid in the vial. Although the result may be imperceptible, the purity is lost. The degree of programming within the individual will determine the extent of contamination of the original purity.

The Pure Channel

To experience the purity in the vial, we must **receive it from its original source within**. The channel we establish through our communication with our Inner Guide, our True Self is the same channel used by the pure liquid light bathing us in the truth of the universe, the heart of which is Love. This is the same process used by the great masters who have left their magnificent legacy of light-filled creations to inspire us to do as they have done and more.

To experience the purity of the liquid light, we must take all the inspired guidance from the outside world that feels harmonic to our individuality, and let it lead us **inside** to the **original source of living truth** which is pure.

We then follow the direction of our own pure Inner Guidance and allow no outside source to dictate its truth to us. For only **we** can see clearly from within, which path, which system, which direction will lead us to our own eventual awakening to the truth. And that truth is our Oneness with the 'All that Is.' It is knowing from within our highest Self this truth which is beyond the intellectual acceptance of ideas flowing **from the mind of others**, no matter how lofty those ideas may seem.

What versus How Thinking

"What" we want is our job. "How to get it" is the responsibility of our Inner Guide.

How often do we hear the words *"ya, but"* after we decide or learn about *"how"* we need to proceed in order to accomplish a given task or goal. This hesitation flows from the existing programming in our inner guidance system which determines what is considered possible, difficult or impossible for us to do.

The source of these prejudgements traces back to our life experiences learned personally or vicariously through the experiences of others. Where there is a similar task or goal in the past in which obstacles occurred and failure at some level resulted, the memory creates a programmed *buffer*, shielding us from experiencing a similar discomfort in the future.

The intensity of our *passion* to achieve our goal determines our fortitude to push past these "ya, but" buffers to move toward our objective. Without sufficient *passion*, the painful inertia of *procrastination* results, fueled in part by these shielding buffers.

Procrastination is an unconscious decision to accept the lesser of two evils; a misguided logic which motivates the delay of the anticipated suffering associated with the past memory versus the insidious pain of guilt related to inaction. This is a choice which invariably intensifies the buffer by expanding the inner feeling of *not being good enough*.

There is little or no conscious thought needed to procrastinate, just an automatic response to the "ya, but" buffer. Although the self help book and video libraries are saturated with *'how to'* information as an approach to achievement in our society, it is by no means the easiest method to obtain what you desire. While no one can argue with the effectiveness of these approaches, our **Inner Guide** has a far easier and fulfilling method.

I call it the **What versus How** method. The process is simple, if not at first easy. With the development of our **telephone** connection to our own **Inner Guide** and the clarity of direction that results, a steady stream of precise instructions, specific to **our** most immediate needs becomes available. It was always there, but without the connection, how would we know?

Our job is to determine *'what'* we want and the job of our **Inner Guide** is to tell us *'how'* **to proceed perfectly** from moment to moment. It will give us this **how to** information flawlessly and continuously if we **never hang up the phone** and always listen.

This is just the opposite of how most people approach a target—always figuring out *'how to'* proceed next and always running into "ya, buts" that confuse and delay successful accomplishment. With sufficient **passion**, success will still follow, but with far more inconvenience and discomfort than may be necessary.

Our own or learned experience also influences the **logic** that guides our own *'how to'* approach to achievement. Our **logic** usually seems practical and even responsible in the moment of decision to act, nevertheless the *'how to'* approach derived from this method often fails to produce the desired results.

With this in mind, I suggest you begin each day with this simple question for your Inner Guide: **Show me what I need to know for my highest purpose today.** For more specific situations ask: **Show me what is the perfect course of action for me to take in the following situation _____.**

From Victim to Creator

When you pick up a newspaper, a magazine or turn on the television, do you feel you are immediately assaulted by a barrage of negativity? And how about those casual conversations at the office, in a coffee shop, at a bus or train station, or in an elevator. Doesn't it usually contain subject matter that validates that we are at the mercy of circumstances and the mysterious 'they'?

Despite the wealth of self help books, tapes, videos, lectures and workshops at our fingertips, the truth is many people still feel like *victims*. There are innumerable forms of fear related to this victim consciousness, but all dovetail back to a few solid beliefs accepted by most people. The foundation that underpins all these beliefs says *there are ceilings* over our heads and *barriers* that surround what is possible for us to have and experience in life.

It also states that *there is not enough* of what is possible to have and experience to go around. Now if we buy into this popular belief, there is a natural tendency toward thinking selfishly, having a *survival of the fittest* attitude of *them or me*, being competitive and in general *looking out for number one*.

This engenders constant fear and anxiety causing us to build fences around our lives and beliefs while *reinforcing the ego's control over our lives*.

Limitation and the fear it engenders is the antithesis of *true abundance*. It is one of the principle weapons in the ego's arsenal and perpetuates a sense of separation from our fellowman. Abundance is one of the primary truths promoted by our Inner Guide inspiring us to *drop our fears* and unite with our fellowman and embrace the highest attributes within us.

When we are fearless, we stand out *like shining examples* of the highest possibilities of mankind and attract and bind all good things to ourselves. This cohesive force is *the glue* that holds the universe together and is the underlying essence of all life. We call this unifying power *Love*.

When we choose to have an attitude of abundance, it immediately intensifies our ability to link with our Inner Guide and be directed by its wise counsel. We literally turn the knob from *channel victim* to *channel creator*. By allowing the poisoning propaganda of channel victim to constantly flow into our minds, we allow programs to be imprinted into our inner guidance system that run over and over again like a cassette tape or CD on constant replay. The screech of its hypnotizing chant continues to echo within our consciousness long after the newspaper has been laid aside or the television switched off.

And all the programs within our inner guidance system attract other programs that vibrate at the same frequency. This attraction *continues to validate* the belief that the programs must be telling the truth. If we think we are unlucky, ugly or a failure, we attract circumstances that *endorse* those beliefs and so the *cycle of limitation* fuels itself.

Our *thoughts are like magnets attracting* the clothes that will fit the mold or frequency of their vibration. If we buy a package of seeds labeled thistles, we are not surprised when we find a crop of thistles have grown where we planted them. If we give architectural plans to a contractor for a bungalow, we do not expect a two-story house to be built from those plans. And if we step off a cliff without a parachute, we should not be surprised when we find ourselves plummeting to the bottom. I know I wouldn't do that more than once!

Energy follows thought and thoughts proceed in the direction we have sent them as surely as a bullet fired from a rifle. If you would like to know what your thoughts were six months, two or three years ago, you only need to take a detached inventory of your life right now.

Where do you live and work? Who do you keep company with? How do you entertain yourself? What projects, hobbies and goals occupy your time? What do you think about? And how much abundance are you experiencing in both your inner and outer worlds? These are the fruits of your past thoughts. For some, the inventory will be dismal and mediocre. For others, it will be a cornucopia of delightful fruits. But what is really exciting is that whatever you have in your life inventory today, you soon discover *you created*.

The good news is, you can change your *future inventory* by changing your present thoughts.

Choose your Thoughts Carefully

Well, that's obvious isn't it? On the surface the flip side is if you don't choose your own circumstances by choosing your own thoughts, your circumstances will be chosen for you by the most predominant ideas you *allow* to play around in your mind.

Advertising and its repetitive messages describe this phenomena well. Have you ever noticed how a new product, such as a breakthrough skin care product or a new kind of beer, seems to show up everywhere when it is first launched.

This is called *spaced repetition* and it literally creates a new program in our inner guidance systems if we allow it to do so. The first time we come into contact with the product, we are drawn to it like a magnet. We may not buy it, but we are thinking about it.

If we don't choose our own thoughts they will be chosen for us.

Here is an example of how the victim consciousness is perpetuated. *We wake up at 7:00 am to an automatic radio alarm and hear about government cutbacks. At breakfast, as we take our first spoonful of cereal, we read on the front page stories about the falling buying power of our currency, unemployment problems and plant closures. We pick up our voice mail messages after getting ready for work and brother Bill, with a wife and four young children, has just lost his job and mother is having heart palpitations worrying about how he is going to keep up with their mortgage payments.*

On the way to work, which is stop and go for an hour, we see three examples of reckless, selfish driving and two people screaming at each other on the side of the road after a fender bender.

We experience these scenarios or others like them every day. If we allow these images to play around in our minds, they become part of our inner guidance system's programs and attract more images that vibrate at the same frequency. So ***how do we prevent this*** from happening? The answer is by ***not trying to prevent it at all!*** What ***we resist, persists***—this is the meaning of ***resist not evil***. It means, allow the images to pass right through your mind and out again.

It does not mean, however, that we become ***indifferent*** to the suffering of our fellowman. It means we consciously rise above the suffering so that we do not become ***emotionally involved as a victim*** in the problem. When we choose to focus on these images from this ***higher point to view, it becomes possible to calmly wrap our emotions with compassion and caring.*** This enables our thoughts to be part of creative solutions. We can use our emotions, guided by ***love***, to solve problems. This is part of what I call ***passion*** and it is the foundation of ***The Fish Story—Part Three***.

I have found this to be a highly **self empowering** way to look at circumstances that are not abundant and do not bring Peace, Love and Joy into my life.

You Can Make a Difference

Making a positive difference in the world and in the lives of others begins and ends with the **passion** to do so. Unlike the Ancient Success Formula described earlier, this requires no creativity and has no timetable or plan attached to it. Neither does this need to be an effort.

What already exists does not need to be created, only **recognized**. Making a positive difference in the world only requires that you **open up to** what already exists and let it **flow in and through** you. All that the world needs to live a life of abundance, wanting for nothing while experiencing peace, love and joy existed before the world was created.

The 'All that Is' **provided abundance for itself** and all that exists within it. There has never been a time when abundance did not exist.

> *We create lack in our lives through the*
> *power of our thoughts. And we do this*
> *because we believe lack exists*
> *where it does not.*

As long as we play **the program of lack** over and over in our minds, we will experience the manifestation of that program in our lives.

The new paradigm, The Fish Story—Part Three, requires that we accept a new vision of reality. Feeding a person a fish does make a difference and we should express our love in that way as long as others live without abundance in their lives. It recognizes that others do not accept that abundance is everywhere, but it does not require us to agree with this false concept. If we do, we add energy to the illusion and help keep it alive.

To teach a person to fish also makes a difference and in any way we can give our talents, energies and resources to this effort, we also make a difference. It, too, recognizes that others believe they must struggle with **an attitude of no pain no gain** to carve out a slice of the **limited resources** they feel are available in a competitive world. But it does not require that we accept this belief in the illusion of limitation.

To live **as the fish**, in conscious awareness that we are a part of the 'All that Is' and of the abundance that is a part of it, is to accept the **new emerging vision**. This "livingness" of the truth of our reality stands as a shining example of the possibility of mankind. It radiates to all the world a powerful influence that helps to shift the paralyzed thinking that accepts lack as a reality in the world.

And by living this vision of truth, we are impervious to the skepticism and scorn of those who will say we are blind to our environment. They will say, "Look around you. Are you blind? Can you not see the suffering in the world?"

> **Perhaps more than any other gift, those who have this new vision see and experience the suffering of mankind.**

When the light of truth is allowed to shine through you, it casts long shadows behind the illusions of the world. These shadows are a constant reminder of the suffering in the world. And while we live in a state of abundant love, the compassion within us that is its offspring experiences that suffering at a deep level.

While living in a state of blissful abundance, the 'All that Is' is less than whole if even one soul within itself does not share in that awareness. Therefore, we must stand firm and **allow the light to shine** within and through us. Not only to keep our own minds constantly illuminated in the truth of abundance, but also **to expose the lie** of limitation to others.

To live in the truth of abundance, we stand as **a shining example** for all to see the possibility of mankind. Therefore, we do not try to change the world because then we must accept that the illusion in it exists. That simply adds energy to the illusion and perpetuates it.

> **We must not resist a lie because in so doing
> we help keep it alive.**

We must give our attention, our passion, our very energy **to the truth** and through this act of love **we give it our life**. We **play the program of reality**, which is an abundant life.

If we <u>want</u> to live **abundantly**, experiencing **'a balanced life, wanting for nothing, and filled with peace, love and joy,'** we must **focus** our attention, our energy and our **life force** upon that concept. The **'All that Is'** will supply the ways and means, the <u>method</u> the direction through your own **Inner Guide**.

In doing this, you follow your **heart's desire** which is the same within all mankind. Only their **destiny**, their <u>how</u> differs from yours.

> **"Seek first the Kingdom of Heaven, and All
> else will be added unto you!"**

EPILOGUE

Imagine you live in a grand palace in the heart of a kingdom situated in the most peaceful, temperate climate zone you can conceive. Mountains of unequaled splendor surround you while giant palm trees rhythmically sway in gentle breezes. There are pools of crystal clear water to swim in formed by gurgling streams that flow and sing their way down from the side of the mountains into the lush valleys below.

Sweet, peaceful music of angelic proportions lingers in the atmosphere and luscious, exotic fruit hangs everywhere from trees. There are endless forms of entertainment, each different from the next. Loving friends are everywhere when you want companionship, and quiet, uplifting serenity is only a thought away when you desire solitude.

There is no pain, no sickness, no hatred, no envy, and no war. Infinite ways to stimulate your creativity and inspire your mind and soul await you. Everywhere there is peace, love and joy.

One day, you and some of your friends hear of a new game that has been created by the wisest in the kingdom. **It is called Forget.** *The wise one has spread the word about this marvelous new game and many are interested in hearing more about it.*

"Wouldn't it be fun," the wise one suggests, "to forget the wonderful blessing of our lives here in the kingdom so that when we remember we will have such a wonderful surprise? It will be a contrast of unparalleled delight."

Contrast *was definitely something new and* **did not exist** *in the beautiful kingdom. Colors, sound, smells, tastes and textures all blended seamlessly into each other without discord of any kind. Contrast would be unique and an experience new to you and your friends.*

You and your friends agreed the game sounded exciting and might be a lot of fun. What could be the harm, you thought. And so it was decided to play the wise one's new game. The wise one then led you and your friends to a steep set of stairs and explained that all you had to do was walk down the steps and you would slowly forget your blissful life in the kingdom.

You all nodded your understanding and, with anticipation, began the long descent with total trust, unaware of any danger. As you advanced deeper and deeper down the stairs, the wise one could be faintly heard in the distance telling you to just walk back up the stairs again when you got to the bottom and your memory would return with the exhilarating feeling of once again experiencing **your true estate in paradise.**

Well, as you have probably guessed, if you forget your wondrous home in the kingdom, you also forget the wise one's instructions for returning to it. And that is exactly what happened. Slowly a foggy confusion enveloped your thoughts and you wondered what you were doing walking down these stairs. You assumed someone must know and so you just kept moving. By the time you reached the bottom, your legs ached and your breathe came in short gasps.

You didn't remember ever feeling tired before, but then you didn't really remember anything beyond descending the long stairway. Towering in front of you and your companions was a gigantic lead door. It radiated a cold, uninviting vibration as you reached for the handle to open it. As you turned the handle, one of the others behind you noticed a sign near the top of the door. Everyone asked what it said. He squinted his eyes and slowly read the sign. It said:

> **This is the gateway to separation and limitation. Enter at your own risk!**

No one knew what "separation, limitation or risk" meant, but most seem to recall the word "enter", so that is what you all did. After you and your friends passed through, the entrance the door closed shut with an ominous thud. Everyone turned with a shock but instead of a door, a beautiful mountain of inconceivable grandeur stood in its place. Something about the magnificent towering peak was familiar, friendly and vaguely reminded you of a place called home.

There was a plaque at the base of the mountain and one of your friends read:

> **"Mount Abundance,**
> **the Passion of Humanity"**

For a moment, you and the others all shared a vision of a beautiful palace in a celestial kingdom and a life filled with abundance of every description. The vision quickly faded and the one who read the writing on the plaque voiced the feelings of all, "Wouldn't it be nice to climb that beautiful mountain some-day? *Abundance sounds like a wonderful dream.*"

The wise one was no where to be seen.

A Year of Inner Guidance

52 Weeks of
Inner Guidance Inspirations

John
McIntosh

A Year of Inner Guidance

52 Weeks of Inner Guidance Inspirations

How to Use These Inspirations

Inner Guidance is a deeply personal thing and suggests direction to our **specific needs at the moment**. The guidance it provides is loving, gentle and infallible. It is **your own personal truth**.

For this reason, following the 52 inspirations chronologically would rarely be in harmony with your personal needs in any particular week.

Allowing your Inner Guide to **choose the correct inspiration for the week** will ensure the closest possible harmonic link with your individual needs.

Step #1

At the beginning of each week, take a few moments to choose the Inner Guidance Inspiration you will use as a **FOCUS** for the week. This choice is made by your Inner Guide in the following way:

Step #2

Allow your mind to drift before you begin. Try not to linger on any one thought.

Step #3

Turn to the pages marked *"My Choice for this Week,"* that are numbered 1 through 52, and pass your finger up and down the line, stopping at the first line that *FEELS* comfortable or *RIGHT* to you.

Step #4

On that line, write the Sunday of that week's date.

Step #5

Turn to the page with the inspiration number for that line and mark it as your *FOCUS* for that week.

Step #6

During the week, read the inspiration at least once a day; aloud is best. Then concisely record any *INSIGHTS* that come to you anytime during the week on the page adjacent to the Inspiration.

This will gradually increase your belief in your Inner Guide as these insights add value to your daily life.

Note: If your Inner Guide chooses the same inspiration *more than once* during the year, just go with it. Not every inspiration may be for you personally.

My Choice for this Week

Inspiration Number   This Week's Date

1   _____

2   _____

3   _____

4   _____

5   _____

6   _____

7   _____

8   _____

9   _____

10   _____

11   _____

12   _____

13   _____

14   _____

15   _____

16   _____

17   _____

18 _____

19 _____

20 _____

21 _____

22 _____

23 _____

24 _____

25 _____

26 _____

27 _____

28 _____

29 _____

30 _____

31 _____

32 _____

33 _____

34 _____

35 _____

36 _____

37 _____

38 _____

40 _____

41 _____

42 _____

43 _____

44 _____

45 _____

46 _____

47 _____

48 _____

49 _____

50 _____

51 _____

52 _____

INSPIRATION 1

LIFE'S LESSONS

Most of the important lessons I have learned have been those I learned while teaching others. They were not part of the agenda but slipped quietly into my conversation, uninvited but welcome.

And my greatest teachers have been those people and circumstances that upset me the most. They had the power to agitate unneeded, crystallized thoughts and habits bringing them to the surface and opening my eyes to their presence within me.

This week's Insights:

_____

_____

_____

_____

_____

_____

_____

_____

_____

_____

_____

_____

_____

_____

_____

_____

_____

INSPIRATION 2

FREEDOM

I have observed a little of the purity and magic of life by watching children from a distance. They live life the way grown ups would live if they moved with the perfect rhythm that animates the universe.

There is a similarity between nature and children, a spontaneity that responds instantly to inner guidance. There is a succession of joyful activities, gestures, expressions and deep thoughtful insights in their innocent eyes.

The freedom with which they approach each new thing they find is complete and unhindered by the cacophony of anxious thoughts that tug at our so-called mature minds.

This week's Insights

_____
_____
_____
_____
_____
_____
_____
_____
_____
_____

INSPIRATION 3

TRUTH

What is Truth that it is so easily molded to one's affection? Can we color the wind to our liking? I think not!

The embellishment of one's own designs to fit the pattern of the cloak, stretches the fabric that at some time of inordinate pressure, tears at its weakest points and thereby reveals the inconsistency.

I am no longer persuaded that the ends justify the means; experience has killed this poor excuse.

When viewed from a great height, it becomes clear. Truth has a subtle but vital and patient life of its own, which straightens crooked places and blends the colors of deceit into crystal clarity, no matter how enduring the stitch that holds the lie.

This week's Insights

_____

_____

_____

_____

_____

_____

_____

_____

_____

_____

INSPIRATION 4

TIME

Time marches on relentlessly and the body gives up its youthfulness, but the mind may rise or fall and live in the age of its choosing.

Abundance and joy are mixed with cruel challenges and sorrows, but through all the tests of life, Love endures throughout the ages.

This week's Insights

_____

_____

_____

_____

_____

_____

_____

_____

_____

_____

_____

_____

_____

_____

_____

_____

_____

_____

INSPIRATION 5

LOVE

All the happiness from trials overcome,
And pleasure deep from achievements won,

Touch the mind and leave a trace,
Of fleeting Peace And Joy's embrace.

But only Love that holds no strings,
Can leave the Joy no thing can bring.

May God enrich the Love we share,
And spread it wide from hearts that care.

This week's Insights

_____
_____
_____
_____
_____
_____
_____
_____
_____
_____
_____
_____
_____
_____
_____
_____

INSPIRATION 6

OPINION AND SILENCE

Unseen forces like wind, heat and cold are marvelous aren't they? We see the effects of these forces but not the forces themselves.

Take silence for example; I have found it has a wonderfully neutralizing effect on opinions.

This week's Insights

_____
_____
_____
_____
_____
_____
_____
_____
_____
_____
_____
_____
_____
_____
_____
_____
_____
_____
_____

Inspiration 7

Thoughts

I'm sure you've noticed how constantly held thoughts eventually come into being. If that is true, why do we settle for so many little ones?

This week's Insights

_____

_____

_____

_____

_____

_____

_____

_____

_____

_____

_____

_____

_____

_____

_____

_____

_____

_____

_____

_____

_____

Inspiration 8

Truth Found in Union

As false and Truth unite, that which is illusion falls away, darkness disappears into Light.

The more we look at the fear in darkness, the less we see it, and the clearer Truth becomes beneath its surface. Therefore, face fear and it will disappear.

This week's Insight

INSPIRATION 9

POINTS OF VIEW

I have discovered my point of view changes as my attitude rises. Like a helicopter rising above a raging river only to find it becomes a placid stream just a little ways ahead.

This week's Insights

_____
_____
_____
_____
_____
_____
_____
_____
_____
_____
_____
_____
_____
_____
_____
_____
_____
_____
_____
_____
_____
_____

INSPIRATION 10
THE ILLUSION OF FAILURE

I believe none of us ever fails at anything. Every time we create something we are successful at creation. However, we do make some poor choices about what we create.

This week's Insights

_____

_____

_____

_____

_____

_____

_____

_____

_____

_____

_____

_____

_____

_____

_____

_____

_____

_____

_____

_____

INSPIRATION 11

CHANGING TIMES

I believe we are living in the most wonderful time in history for those who seek the highest within themselves.

The dividing line between darkness and light is more apparent each day and brings with it a clarity of purpose and direction.

As the pockets of light now shining everywhere throughout the world grow in brilliance, they silhouette long shadows behind the stumbling blocks to growth.

And if we dwell on expanding the light that is now becoming so conspicuous, and not judging the shadows, we will quickly become one with it.

This week's Insights

_____

_____

_____

_____

_____

_____

_____

_____

_____

_____

_____

_____

INSPIRATION 12

CHOOSING ABUNDANCE

Abundance is all around us and we experience it every moment. But is it the abundance we really desire?

What has been our primary focus over the last one, two or three years? That is the abundance we now have!

Thoughts of getting out of debt... create abundant debt!

Thoughts of financial independence... create wealth!

Thoughts of getting rid of a thankless job attract another one with a different name!

Thoughts of selflessly serving our fellowman attract a multitude of opportunities for Abundance on every level.

It's our choice.

This week's Insights

_____
_____
_____
_____
_____
_____
_____
_____
_____
_____

INSPIRATION 13

FRUSTRATIONS

I have found irritations are best dissolved through non-resistance. Not that we avoid the responsibility of the issue, we simply don't fight it.

And in this calmer space, our thoughts have clearer vision allowing solutions to flow to us more easily or courage to fortify us if we must endure a little longer.

This week's Insights

_____
_____
_____
_____
_____
_____
_____
_____
_____
_____
_____
_____
_____
_____
_____
_____
_____
_____
_____

Inspiration 14

Balance

Not long ago a good friend told me she was
TIRED BUT WIRED.

I laughed! We all get that way sometimes, <u>exhausted but</u>
<u>exhilarated</u>.

This can be a wonderful blush after a day well spent. It
can also be <u>fatigue</u> and <u>irritation</u> from a poorly balanced
day of high activity and little productivity.

Are we overly concerned with appearances or actively
engaged in following our heart's desire?

I have found a few minutes of early morning
introspection can provide the balance that makes the
difference at day's end.

This week's Insights

_____
_____
_____
_____
_____
_____
_____
_____
_____
_____
_____

INSPIRATION 15

PATIENCE

Have you noticed how a thing done often becomes easier to do, even hard not to do? It's like a groove—hard to start but simple to follow once started. Patience is like that!

This week's Insights

_____

_____

_____

_____

_____

_____

_____

_____

_____

_____

_____

_____

_____

_____

_____

_____

_____

_____

_____

_____

INSPIRATION 16

INSPIRATION

A baby's soul descends into the planes of matter blessing its family with light and drawing heaven a little closer.

Inspiration is like that—a heavenly experience that transcends normal thinking.

It springs forth from a profound sense of desire to create and seems to open a channel that stimulates the mind with ideas and fuels the fires within to take action.

This week's Insights

_____

_____

_____

_____

_____

_____

_____

_____

_____

_____

_____

_____

_____

_____

_____

_____

INSPIRATION 17

FINE TUNING

A wise man once said, "It is the small refinements of something good that makes it great!"

How true! Grand splashes and thundering achievements are in the minority.

Most of a life intent on excellence is a series of 'baby steps,' gradually and steadily honing and perfecting worthy ideals. It is a process of chipping away the excess baggage of imperfection to find the exquisite statue that already exists within.

This week's Insights

_____

_____

_____

_____

_____

_____

_____

_____

_____

_____

_____

_____

_____

_____

_____

INSPIRATION 18

THE VALUE OF STRESS

When I was very young I noticed how much more force water had as long as I pressed my thumb against the nozzle of a garden hose. Later I learned stress creates many opportunities for us to grow faster provided we don't quit.

This week's Insights

_____

_____

_____

_____

_____

_____

_____

_____

_____

_____

_____

_____

_____

_____

_____

_____

_____

_____

_____

INSPIRATION 19

FORGIVENESS

Nothing frees the mind and lifts the spirit like forgiveness. And if the mind is free so follows the body.

The things we will not forgive remain attached to us intensifying the original wounds and exaggerating them.

Let us then heal ourselves and regain our freedom by forgiving quickly new as well as old wounds, and let us begin by forgiving ourselves.

This week's Insights

_____

_____

_____

_____

_____

_____

_____

_____

_____

_____

_____

_____

_____

_____

_____

_____

_____

_____

INSPIRATION 20

SELF ESTEEM

Self esteem is like a magnet. It creates a sense of worthiness that attracts abundance.

This week's Insights

_____

_____

_____

_____

_____

_____

_____

_____

_____

_____

_____

_____

_____

_____

_____

_____

_____

_____

_____

_____

_____

_____

INSPIRATION 21

LUCK

The cycle of service is infallible if not predictable. The service we perform arcs out into the universe returning to us full measure what we have given.

However, it often wears a disguise on its return and will frequently appear as luck when it returns wearing different clothes from those we dressed it in.

Nevertheless, the luck was earned. And so, to be constantly lucky we must be constantly serving.

This week's Insights

_____
_____
_____
_____
_____
_____
_____
_____
_____
_____
_____
_____
_____
_____
_____
_____
_____

Inspiration 22

Peace

The world's chaos swirls around us, but remain centered in peace,

Distractions challenge the mind from every direction. Still, remain focused in tranquillity.

Illusions assault our every sense and the school of life does its bitter-sweet dance. But obey the voice of silence within and calming waves of serenity sweep over us.

This week's Insights

INSPIRATION 23

TRUST

Let our defensive walls collapse under the precious white snows of Trust,

Let us not fear the barbs of rejection nor count the many thorns of illusions that never come,

Let flow the gentle stream of Love and return to the Peace that lies within.

This week's Insights

_____

_____

_____

_____

_____

_____

_____

_____

_____

_____

_____

_____

_____

_____

_____

_____

_____

_____

_____

_____

Inspiration 24

Reality

As we approach each success in our destiny the miracles that surround us become visible and we wonder how we forgot they were always there.

This week's Insights

_____

_____

_____

_____

_____

_____

_____

_____

_____

_____

_____

_____

_____

_____

_____

_____

_____

_____

_____

_____

_____

_____

INSPIRATION 25

ON TRACK

Most of my life has been spent in a kind of foggy search, bumping into walls, taking detours and spending years on what seemed the wrong paths.

And yet, although I have mostly chosen the hard road, at last, as each facet of the diamond of awareness reveals itself to me, I find I have just been on a wide orbit, never out of the perfectly balanced swing around the Light of Truth

How great are the inner workings of truth and how patient its wait for our awakening.

This week's Insights

_____

_____

_____

_____

_____

_____

_____

_____

_____

_____

_____

_____

_____

_____

INSPIRATION 26

A LIFE OF JOY

A life of Joy that, if we will, can fill our hearts and warm the chill, that pressures bring and problems heavy, have cooled the world, to blessings many.

May smiles that glow and hearts that give, allow the Love we wish to live, spread not to few or those that flatter, but to great and small, for all should matter.

This week's Insights

_____

_____

_____

_____

_____

_____

_____

_____

_____

_____

_____

_____

_____

_____

_____

_____

_____

_____

_____

INSPIRATION 27

THE INNER GUIDE

Hunches, insights, flashes, gut feelings and intuition are all helpful telephone calls from our Inner Guide.

They come, it would seem, haphazardly.

In reality, they are steady streams of wise and loving direction always available to us,

If only we will not hang up the phone.

This week's Insights

_____

_____

_____

_____

_____

_____

_____

_____

_____

_____

_____

_____

_____

_____

_____

_____

_____

_____

INSPIRATION 28

KINDNESS

Kindness is like a magical mirror that instantly shows us the best of what we are inside.

This week's Insights

_____

_____

_____

_____

_____

_____

_____

_____

_____

_____

_____

_____

_____

_____

_____

_____

_____

_____

_____

_____

_____

INSPIRATION 29

UNSEEN GROWTH

In the face of reason flies the mystery of chaos. Yet out of chaos came Light.

Let us then accept the hidden magic of Spirit's wisdom having faith in the silent growth that moves in our darkest hours.

This week's Insights

_____

_____

_____

_____

_____

_____

_____

_____

_____

_____

_____

_____

_____

_____

_____

_____

_____

_____

_____

_____

INSPIRATION 30

ASPIRATION

Let us yield to the highest that is within us. Let us think lofty thoughts that light our minds and expose the darkness in our world.

Let us be the best we can be and stand as shining examples for others to follow.

And let us grow in equal humility as we grow in power that our influence will create a harvest of Gentleness and Love.

This week's Insights

_____
_____
_____
_____
_____
_____
_____
_____
_____
_____
_____
_____
_____
_____
_____

INSPIRATION 31
PASSIVE POWER

That which we resist, persists!

The force of any opponent is conquered best by its own weight if we let go and go with the flow. Therefore, let us resist not our challenges but rise above them as the fire of their antagonism is extinguished by our calm.

This week's Insights

_____
_____
_____
_____
_____
_____
_____
_____
_____
_____
_____
_____
_____
_____
_____
_____
_____
_____
_____

Inspiration 32

The Courage of Love

If a younger brother plays with matches, do we wait until he burns down the house before we correct his mistakes?

By then we have suffered serious injury that may inhibit our ability to forgive!

Love must have the courage to correct a loved one before the damage is too great to repair.

And if the brother is dull and at first does not hear our counsel, the courage of Love must persist until our brother listens and learns.

This week's Insights

_____

_____

_____

_____

_____

_____

_____

_____

_____

_____

_____

_____

_____

_____

INSPIRATION 33

DETACHMENT

Who is the master and who is the servant?

Do we bend in agony at the loss of power or possessions? And do we puff up at their acquisition?

True Peace can only be achieved when we want for nothing.

Let us begin by being detached from all we now possess.

This week's Insights

_____

_____

_____

_____

_____

_____

_____

_____

_____

_____

_____

_____

_____

_____

_____

_____

_____

_____

_____

Inspiration 34

Grief

*Of all the experiences in life, nothing has drawn me
inside for guidance and comfort more than grief.*

This week's Insights

_____
_____
_____
_____
_____
_____
_____
_____
_____
_____
_____
_____
_____
_____
_____
_____
_____
_____
_____
_____
_____
_____
_____
_____

INSPIRATION 35

INNER GUIDANCE

The direction of Inner Guidance is much different from the step by step linear approach to life we learned

It always suggests we move in an organic fashion, much like the growth of plants. This way of living is like a jigsaw puzzle having no basic pattern given. The pieces are given to us one or two at a time, but do not reveal the final picture until almost complete. When we begin to live this way, very little seems to fit or make sense.

We must learn to <u>feel</u> where the next piece goes. Living this way is difficult at first and requires faith that the direction we are receiving will truly benefit our life. But when we do follow our Inner Guide, things very soon begin to fall into the right place at the right time and life begins to flow without struggle.

This week's Insights

_____

_____

_____

_____

_____

_____

_____

_____

_____

_____

INSPIRATION 36

CHANGING OURSELVES, CHANGES THE WORLD

A light bulb exerts no effort to remove darkness. It just shines! It allows energy to flow through it and do the work.

Likewise, if we are to make positive changes in the world, we need not struggle to do so.

We need only allow the energy of right thinking to animate our thoughts, words and deeds, and the light in our living expression of this right thinking will remove darkness wherever we go and to whomever we touch.

This week's Insights

_____

_____

_____

_____

_____

_____

_____

_____

_____

_____

_____

_____

_____

_____

INSPIRATION 37

CHALLENGES

All challenges are part of the "School of Life"—they do not educate us to become something more than we are.

They give us the opportunity to stretch our awareness that we may remember who we are already.

We are co-creators with Spirit, with "The All that Is."

But our creations are less than perfect and whole because we have forgotten who we are.

Let us embrace our obstacles and challenges and give thanks for each opportunity we are given to wake up.

This week's Insights

_____

_____

_____

_____

_____

_____

_____

_____

_____

_____

_____

_____

_____

_____

INSPIRATION **38**

REJECTION IS REALLY RE-DIRECTION

What is a mouse doing in a maze? Looking for the cheese, right? Each wall he reaches could be thought of as a rejection.

But the simple mind of the mouse sees the wall as re-direction to the food he smells.

Our egos sees the walls as Rejection! But a higher source, our Inner Guide, knows where the perfect food for our needs is waiting.

Eventually, we will find that perfect food, either by believing there are walls and painfully bumping into them, or by listening to our Inner Guide and accepting them as friendly re-direction.

This week's Insights

_____

_____

_____

_____

_____

_____

_____

_____

_____

_____

INSPIRATION 39

WHAT DO WE REALLY WANT?

After the exotic cars, the opulent houses, the first class trips, the designer clothes, the exclusive clubs, the delectable food, and the money...

After all those things and more, what are we really looking for?

If we peel away these fancy coverings, beyond our basic daily needs, we will find the answer.

And if we are honest with ourselves, we will see it immediately.

We want peace and joy and balance surrounded by Love.

How much more quickly and less painfully could we achieve these things if we gave them our primary energy, focus and passion?

Then everything else we obtain, be it great or small will have deeper value to us being built on a rock foundation.

This week's Insights

_____

_____

_____

_____

_____

_____

_____

Inspiration 40

Devotion

When the fire has burned itself out, when the seductive veils of life no longer distract us,

When the need to be needed slips beneath the waves of selflessness, a new light emerges.

I have seen it in the eyes of elderly couples invisibly joined at the heart and soul through a Oneness of spirit.

Let us not wait so long to share our devotion with our fellowman.

This week's Insights

_____

_____

_____

_____

_____

_____

_____

_____

_____

_____

_____

_____

_____

_____

_____

_____

_____

INSPIRATION 41

ABUNDANT LOVE

*When does kindness begin? To withhold it for a day or
even a moment leaves our spirit wanting. Do we fear
what we give away will never return?*

*But fear not! There is not enough room to hold the
abundant love that comes back to us when we give
without conditions.*

This week's Insights

_____

_____

_____

_____

_____

_____

_____

_____

_____

_____

_____

_____

_____

_____

_____

_____

_____

_____

_____

INSPIRATION 42

REFLECTION

Quiet time to go within can save much regret. It can show us clearly where we have been, gently guiding us and illuminating the perfect steps we should take next.

It also develops patience, and the reward of patience is greater patience. Much is missed by submitting to impulses, which is used by the ego to create chaos, discord and separation.

Let us be patient and reflect before we act thereby attracting greater peace into our lives.

This week's Insights

_____

_____

_____

_____

_____

_____

_____

_____

_____

_____

_____

_____

_____

_____

INSPIRATION 43

FRIENDSHIP

Is there a warmer feeling than people sharing, cooperating, compromising, and loving each other?

When we no longer see the ugliness or beauty of another's body, when the warts and scars of a personality that differs from our own no longer sways our affections, when we are content to sit in silence with another human being and feel complete and satisfied, when we rejoice at the opportunity to bring joy to another,

We have found the gift and true meaning of Friendship.

This week's Insights

_____
_____
_____
_____
_____
_____
_____
_____
_____
_____
_____
_____
_____
_____
_____
_____

INSPIRATION 44

ASPIRATION

Nothing stirs the soul more than a burning desire borne in the depths of one's heart.

It conquers doubts and gives courage to rise above the thousand distractions that challenge a worthy ideal.

Faint hearts and inconsistent effort begin with poor commitment.

The solution is always found in aspiring to only that which truly inspires us.

Let us therefore seek out those things before we begin the task of pursuing any goal and our success will be certain.

This week's Insights

_____

_____

_____

_____

_____

_____

_____

_____

_____

_____

_____

_____

INSPIRATION 45

MIRACLES

What we see as miracles are examples of life beyond the veil of illusion.

When we have let the mask of poverty drop from our minds, when we have accepted health and wholeness as our natural state of being, when we have left the sharp tongue of judgement fall from our memory, and when we have allowed the healing power of Love to dominate our thoughts, the periodic miracles of life will become everyday life.

This week's Insights

_____
_____
_____
_____
_____
_____
_____
_____
_____
_____
_____
_____
_____
_____

INSPIRATION 46

HEALING

The specters of the past take their home in the cells of our body causing discord and disease.

If we would be healed and whole we must release all the lessons that have been learned,

All the vengeful thoughts that are still buried deep within our minds,

All the anxiety and guilt from past mistakes, and every dark memory that still drifts through our sleepless dreams,

Health and well being will find a comfortable home in bodies that are cleansed of the refuse of the past.

This week's Insights

_____

_____

_____

_____

_____

_____

_____

_____

_____

_____

_____

Inspiration 47

Angels all Around Us

Have you heard an Angel's voice sing the praise of music's velvet touch as it breaks through the hardest heart to find what lies within us all?

Have you felt the inspiration of an Angel's gentle persuasion urging you to express the greatest that is within you?

Have you seen the shining beacon of an Angel's towering image set the standard of Courage and Leadership?

Yes, you have! Perhaps you knew and breathlessly embraced the moment. Perhaps you knew it not but loved the blessing you received no less.

Look! They are all around us. Look!

This week's Insights

_____

_____

_____

_____

_____

_____

_____

_____

_____

_____

_____

INSPIRATION 48

TODAY I HAD A DREAM

It was a wonderful dream of life the way I know it soon will be.

There were no wars, no hatred no hunger and no poverty.

Peace prevailed everywhere and all life co-existed in perfect harmony.

Cooperation and creativity were a natural way of living, that all took for granted.

Our Mother Earth was treated as a partner and respected for her life sustaining abundance.

And love floated in the air as a gentle uplifting breeze, subtle, but always there.

No healing was needed since no sickness existed.

Today I had a wonderful dream.

This week's Insights

_____

_____

_____

_____

_____

_____

_____

_____

_____

INSPIRATION 49

GUILT

Guilt is a prison from which abundance is kept without.

The acceptance of unworthiness is the offspring of guilt,

And Unworthiness destroys self esteem.

Without self esteem we close the door to Abundance.

Much effort and many prayers have yielded great fruit in unseen dimensions waiting to manifest in our lives, when we feel we deserve them.

People call it luck when that happens, but the truth is we simply opened to what had already been earned before we closed the door to Abundance through guilt.

Let us forgive ourselves quickly that our lives will become Abundant now!

This week's Insights

_____

_____

_____

_____

_____

_____

_____

_____

_____

_____

INSPIRATION 50

A POINT TO VIEW FROM

A point to view from is different from a point of view. A point of view is an opinion, always influenced by personal prejudices,

A point to view from is vision elevated above a given situation, unattached to its outcome.

It rises above the emotional influence of personal involvement, and sees objectively all sides to the circumstances.

It is possible only when directed by Inner Guidance which is humble, impersonal and always comes from a win-win perspective. And it always promotes Peaceful resolutions.

This week's Insights

_____

_____

_____

_____

_____

_____

_____

_____

_____

_____

_____

INSPIRATION 51

VALUE IN BEING OFF TRACK

Much of our life we seem to be off track.

We zig and we zag from side to side often appearing to go nowhere.

But if we elevate our vision a little we may see the blessing in this picture.

A simple stitch will hold pieces of cloth together but it can be easily broken.

A zig-zag stitch will accomplish the same objective but with more strength. And yet, if you observe the zig-zag stitch it is always headed in the same direction as the straight lined stitch... but in its off track procedure was far stronger than the direct course.

This week's Insights

_____
_____
_____
_____
_____
_____
_____
_____
_____
_____
_____

Inspiration 52

What or How?

What do you think about most often, WHAT you want, or HOW to get it?

And if it's HOW to get it, do you also think how not to get it?

Why you're not good enough, not experienced enough, nor intelligent enough, or the wrong age, wrong color or wrong sex?

But if you focus your thoughts on WHAT you want and go within for the HOW, Miracles happen often that make the WHAT possible to everyone.

This week's Insights

_____

_____

_____

_____

_____

_____

_____

_____

_____

_____

_____

_____

_____

About the Author

John McIntosh has been an entrepreneur and leader in the field of sales management, marketing, training and motivation for 31 years. During that time he has risen to the level of national sales manager in two separate companies, founded two companies for which he acted as president, and for the last 15 years, together with his wife, has operated a highly successful, international natural health company.

Over the last 25 years, he has trained thousands of salespeople internationally presenting his material with high energy and conviction based on personal experience and success.

He has been a student of motivational and spiritual philosophy during his entire career, successfully incorporating the ideas he learned into his own daily life and his inspirational training. His success has led him to the summit in a highly competitive industry. It has provided him with a lifestyle of freedom in both inner and outer worlds based on a strong foundation of Inner Guidance.

In 1996, he wrote a novel on the subject of Abundant Living

through Inner Guidance called ***The Millennium Tablets***. In 1997, John acted as editor and ghost writer for ***The Keys to The Kingdom*** by his long-time mentor, Edith Bruce.

John also publishes a daily ***Inner Guidance Inspiration*** and distributes through e-mail. To subscribe, e-mail:

john@innerguidance.com

Subject: Daily Inspiration

Message: Subscribe

To learn about John McIntosh's ***workshops on "Living Abundantly through Inner Guidance,"*** you may contact the author in the following ways:

Toll Free at: 1-800-838-7114

E-mail: john@innerguidance.com

Fax: (613) 267-0003

or visit the Inner Guidance Web Site at:

www.innerguidance.com/innerguidance

WHAT OTHERS ARE SAYING ABOUT JOHN MCINTOSH

"Thank you for your direction and leadership. Your workshop was excellent."
  —Lyle Thorpe, Mara, British Columbia

"John, I want to let you know how much I appreciate your inspiring leadership and how lucky I was to have attended this special event."
  —Wendy Spencer, Calgary, Alberta

"We received some excellent ideas from you, John, and your discussion was just what we needed."
  —Jim and Marianne Barickman, Citrus Heights,
    California

"Thank you, John, so much. I will never forget this life changing event."
  —Leona Magnan, Calgary, Alberta

"John, your book, *The Millennium Tablets,* is truly life
awakening and uplifting."
    —Bill and Clem Herron, Brandon, Mississippi

"I want to thank you for the seminar last weekend. It really
impacted me in so many ways!"
    —Maggie Olund, Phoenix, Arizona

"I enjoyed your book immensely. I found the story woven
together into a loom of thought with sound, color and light."
    —Donna Hurford, Toronto, Ontario

"It was a real pleasure spending time with you in Hawaii and
speaking with you. I especially appreciate your insight into
my future with the gifts you feel I have."
    —Sharon Peterman, Spokane, Washington

"I really enjoyed *The Millennium Tablets*, John. Thank you."
    —Andrea Williams, Australia

"Your book, *The Millennium Tablets*, is an intriguing
adventure similar to *The Celestine Prophesy* and *Queen of
The Sun.*
    —Byron Kirkwood, Bunch, Oklahoma
        Author of *Survival Guide for the New Millennium*
        (Blue Dolphin Publishing)

"John delivered a series of lectures on *Effective Persuasion* here
at Ryerson. He held the students enthralled. The uniqueness
of his subject matter, approach and delivery contributed to a
rapport with the students that was most unusual."
    —*E. W. Collins, Ryerson Polytechnical Institute, Toronto,
    Ontario*

The force of evil is conscious of its imminent loss of power over the material world. During these last few critical years before the millennium it will take the greatest commitment of the force of light to stave off the real danger of delaying the Age of Light for another eon.

THE MILLENNIUM TABLETS

The Quest for Light

John McIntosh

Also by John McIntosh

A near-death experience takes world famous architect Jonathan King through a series of life-changing events placing the prophetic power of The Millennium Tablets in his hands. With The Millennium Tablets comes a profound choice he must make that could change the course of his life forever and influence the direction of millions of other lives.

$19.95 (plus S&H)

To order a copy of *The Millennium Tablets*:

Call: 1-800-838-7114, or

Logon to: http://www.innerguidance.com/innerguidance/
    millenniumtabletsstage.html